I hope you have a wonderful Christmas.

I hope you get all the things on your wish-list.

This time of year brings peace and joy.

Give to the less fortunate girls and boys.

Lets say a prayer for those who are not here.

Be grateful we made it to the end of the year.

I hope your Christmas is colorful and bright.

I hope your Christmas tree is pretty with lights.

I hope your ornaments fill your tree. .

Merry Christmas from Miss Dejha B!

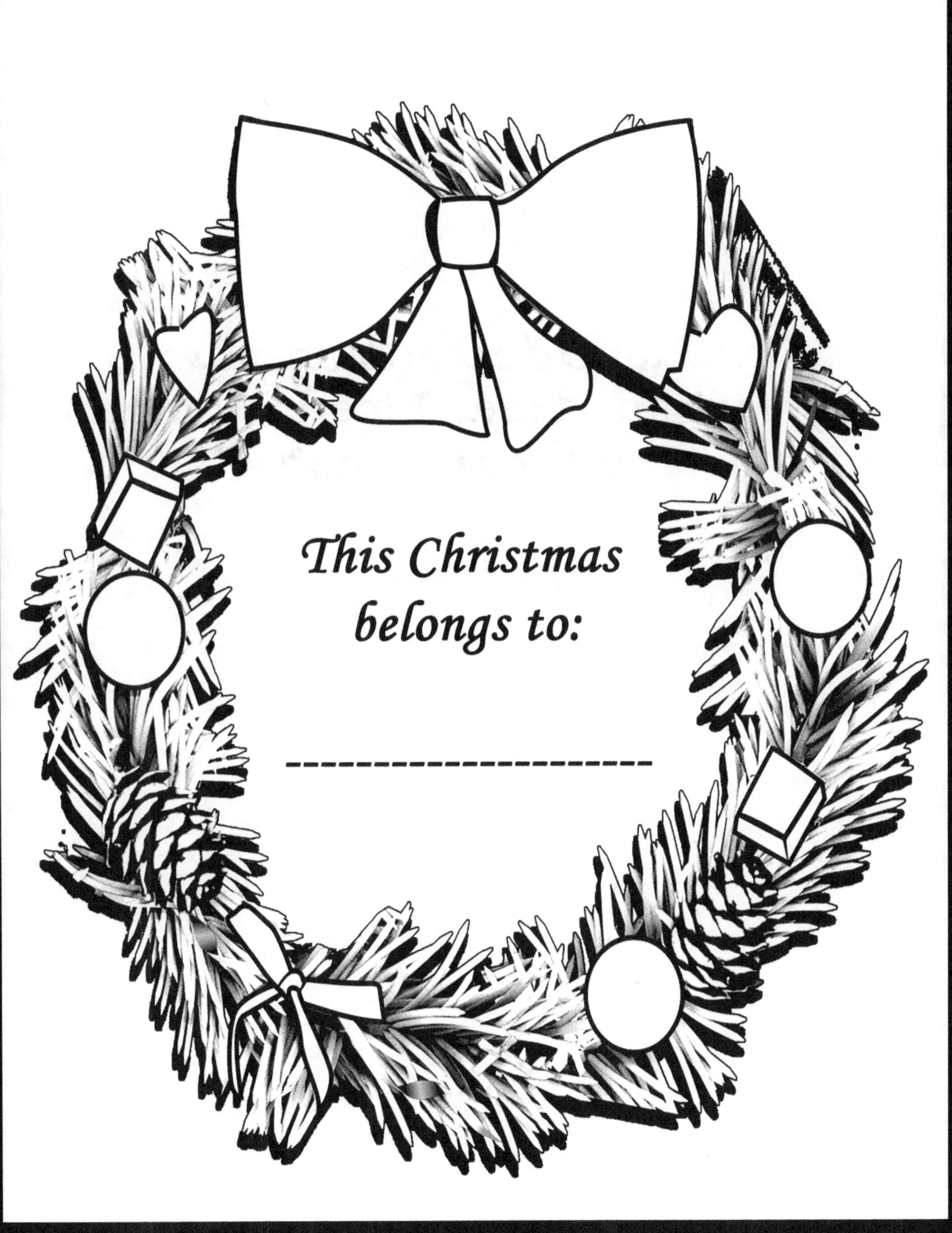

This Christmas
belongs to:

I love decorating my Christmas tree. Once it's done it will look pretty!

Wishing You a Merry Christmas

This year were you
naughty or nice?

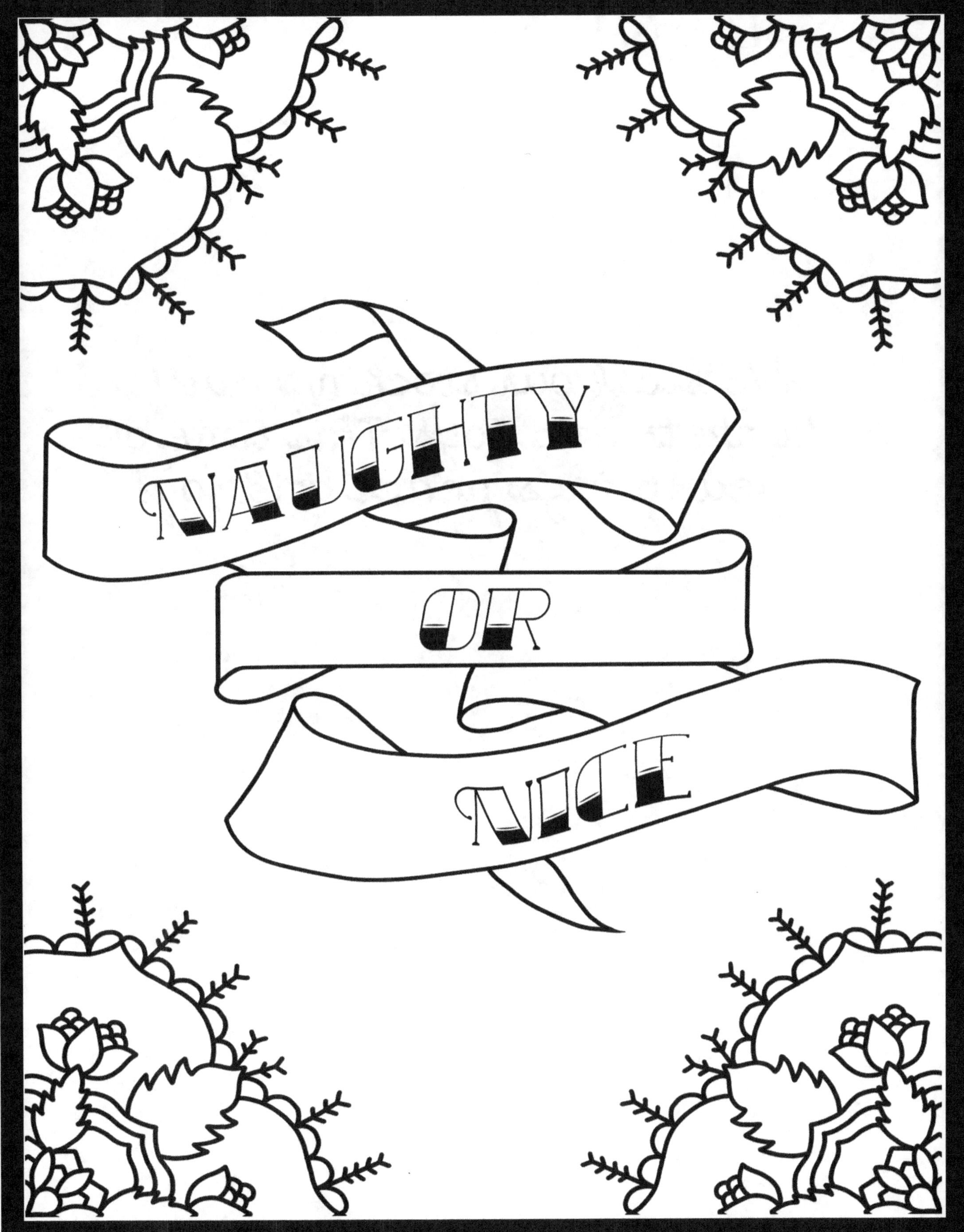

NAUGHTY
OR
NICE

WE stuff our stockings with trinkets and toys. This time of year brings peace and joy!

12 Days Until Christmas

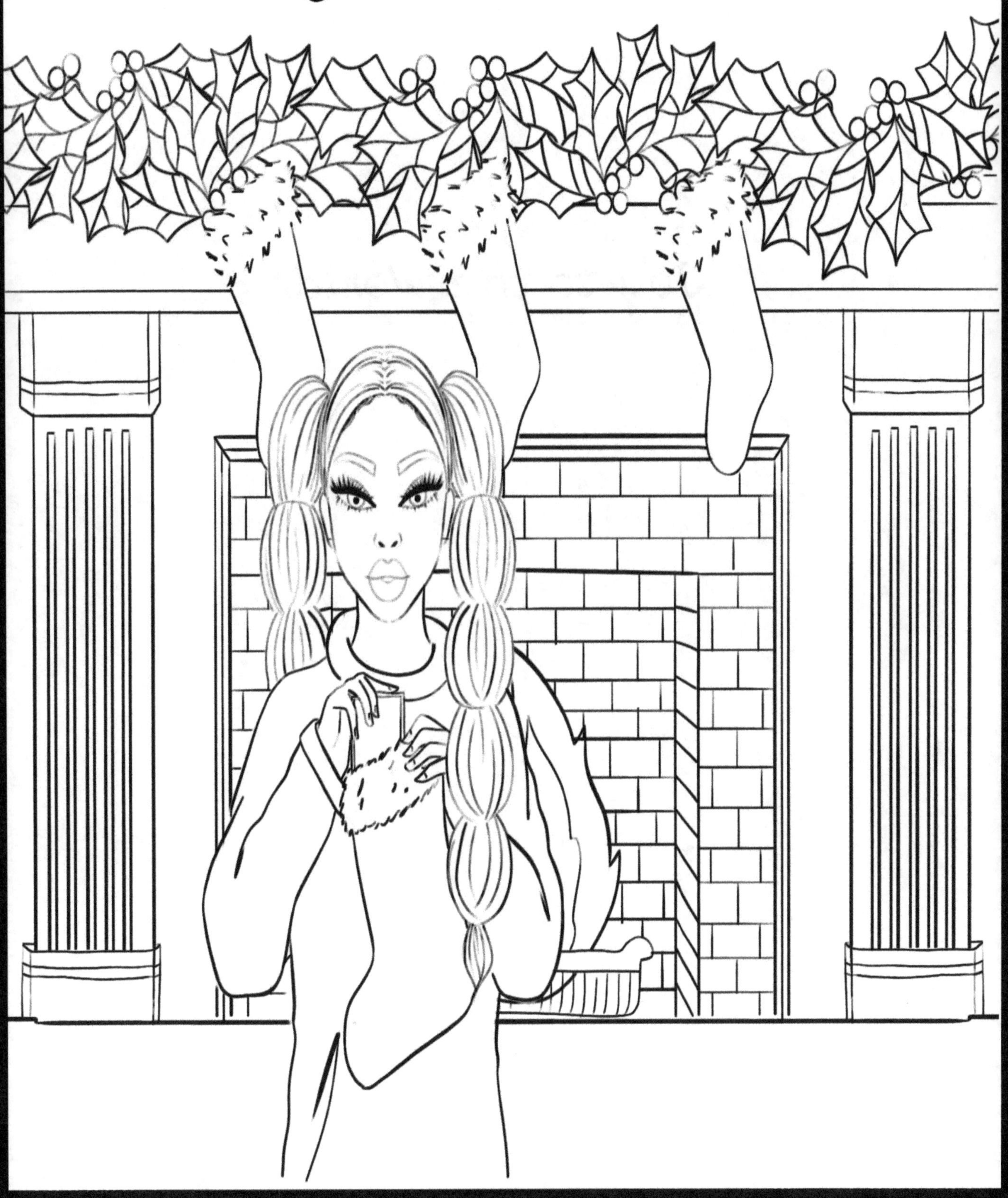

Joy to the World!

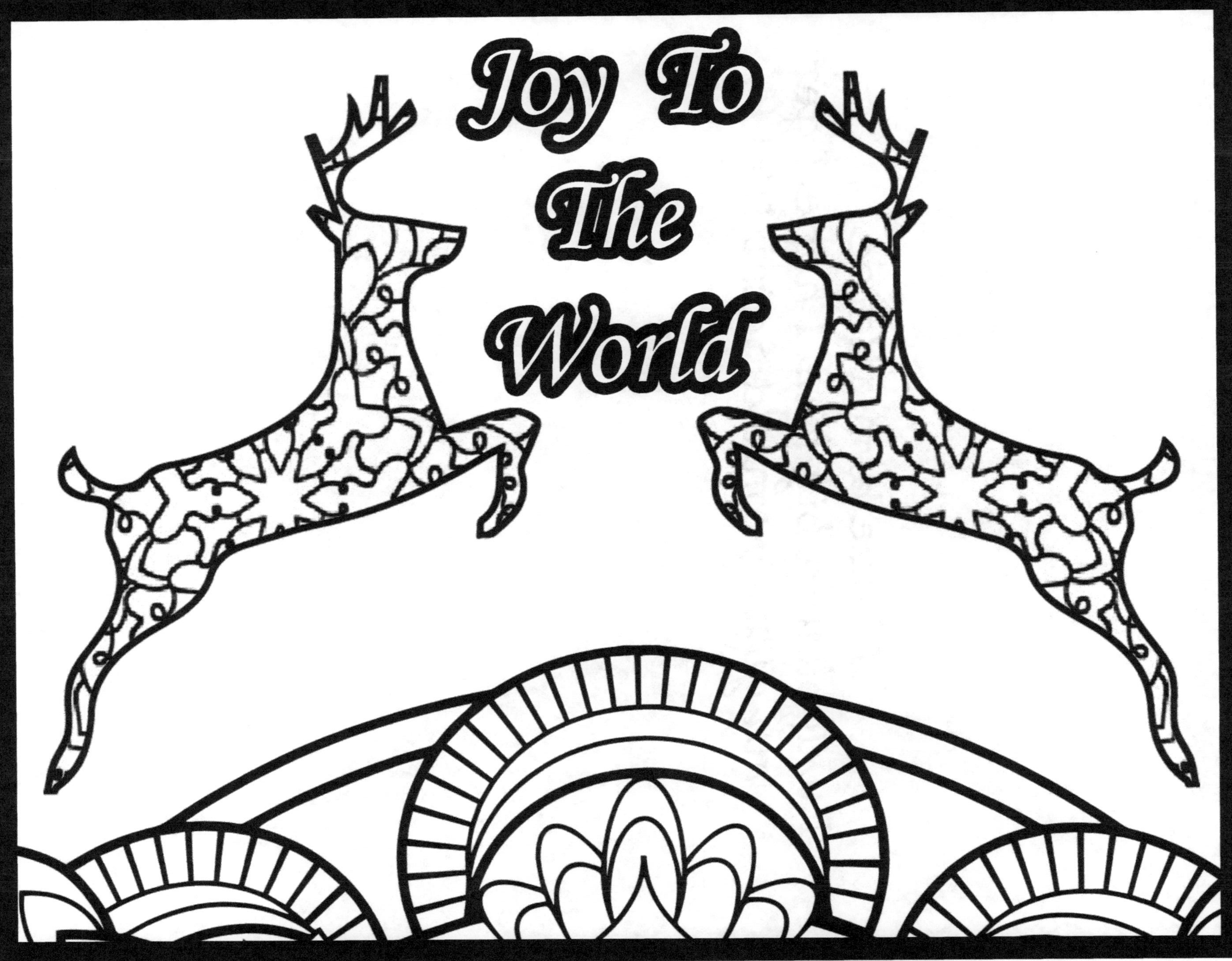

Joy To
The
World

I have a mistletoe
I will blow a big kiss. I hope I get
my gifts from old Saint Nick!

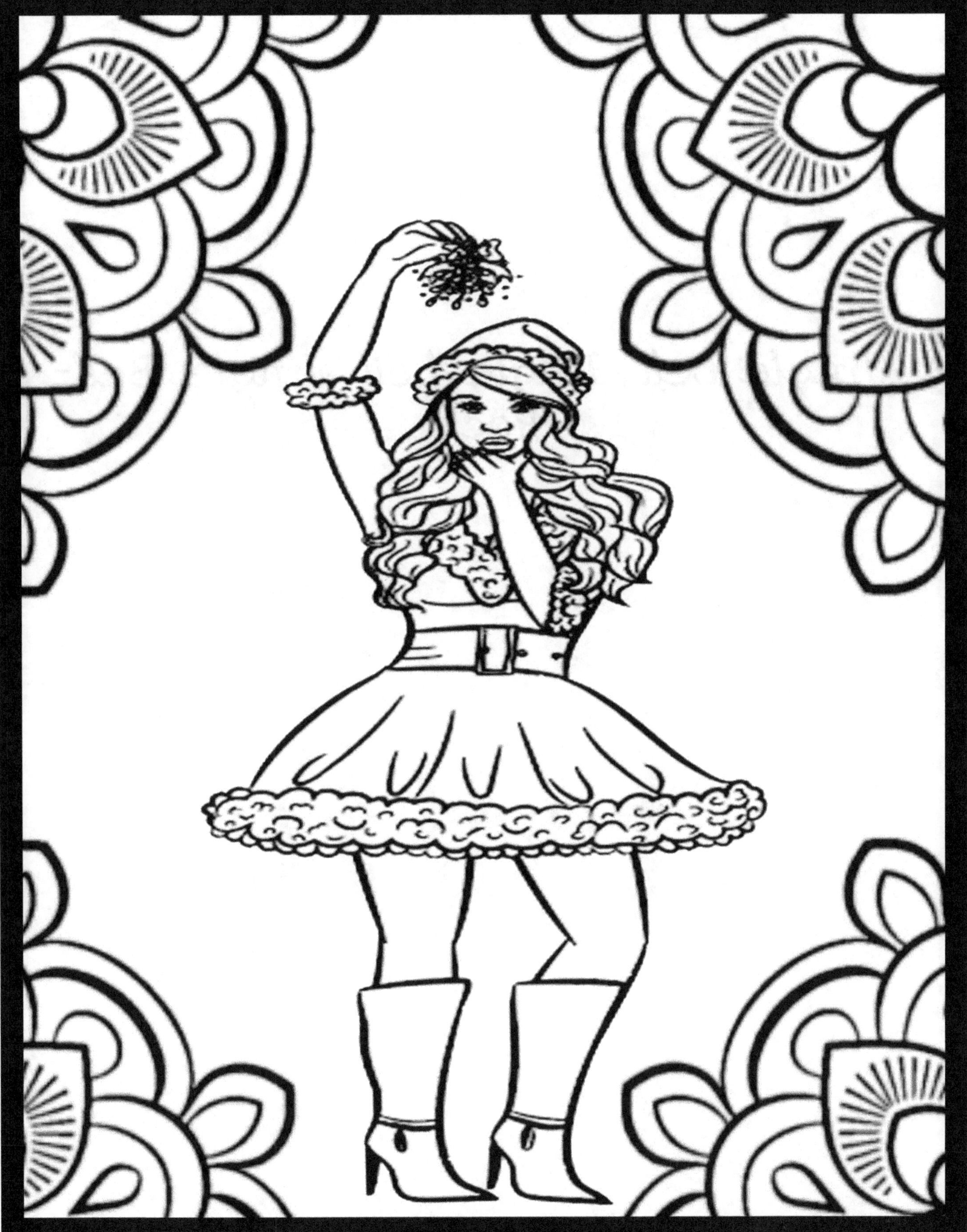

Jingle bell Jingle bell Jingle Bell-
Rock....

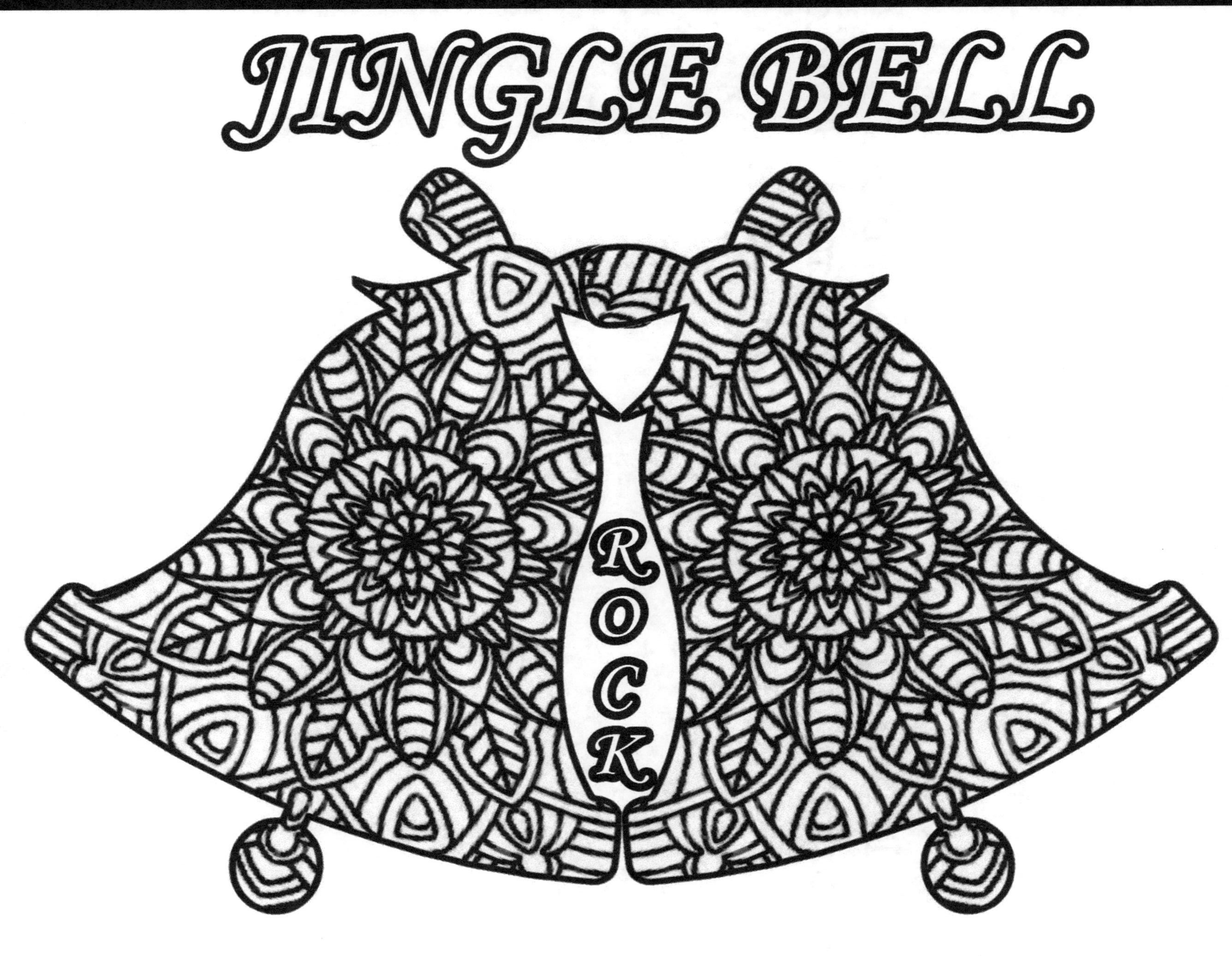

JINGLE BELL
ROCK

Drinking hot chocolate makes
me warm and nice. Sometimes I add
some sugar and spice.

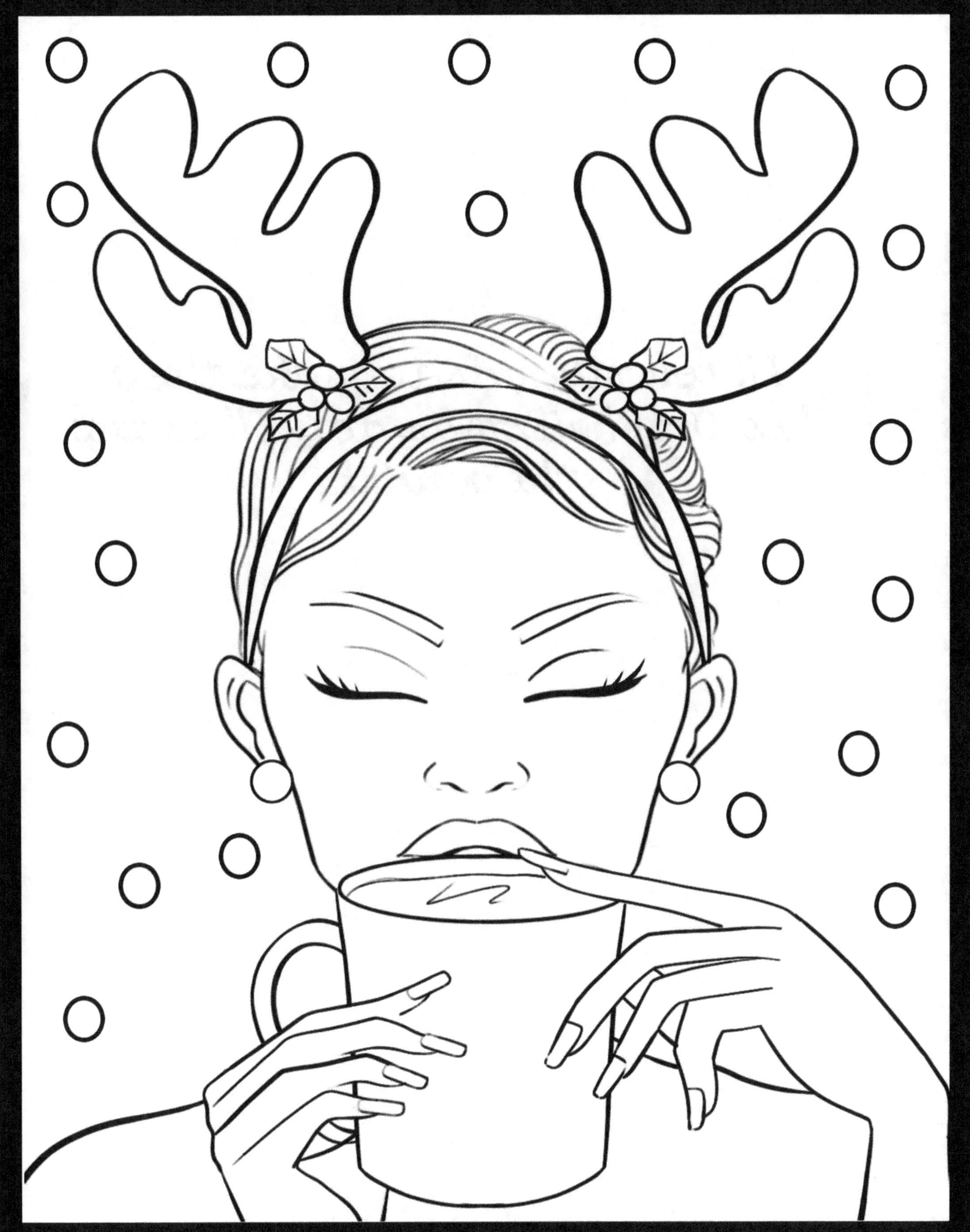

I'll tell my kids to make their list. On Christmas day I'll grant their wish!

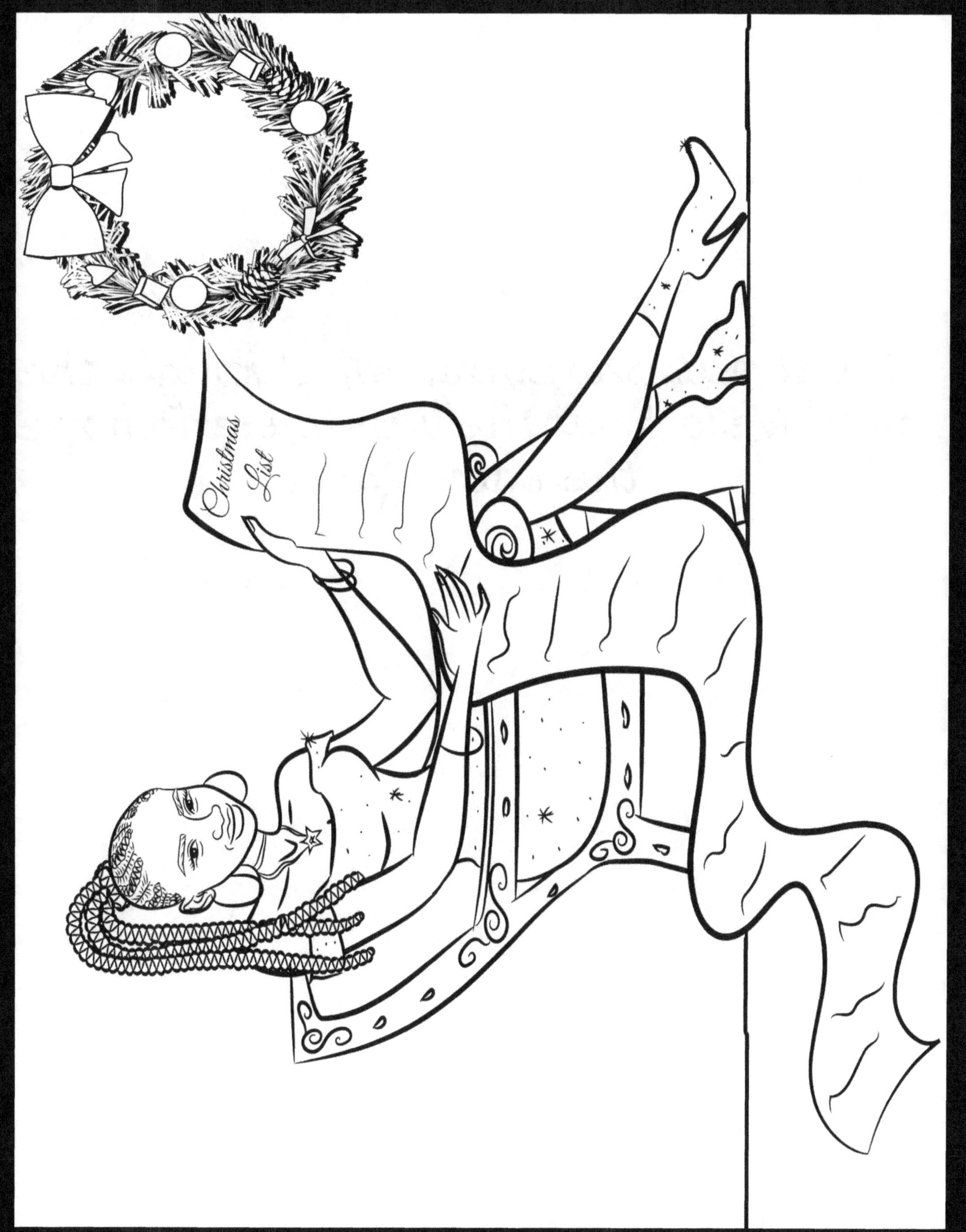
Christmas List

Christmas shopping all through the mall. We look out the window and hope the snow falls.

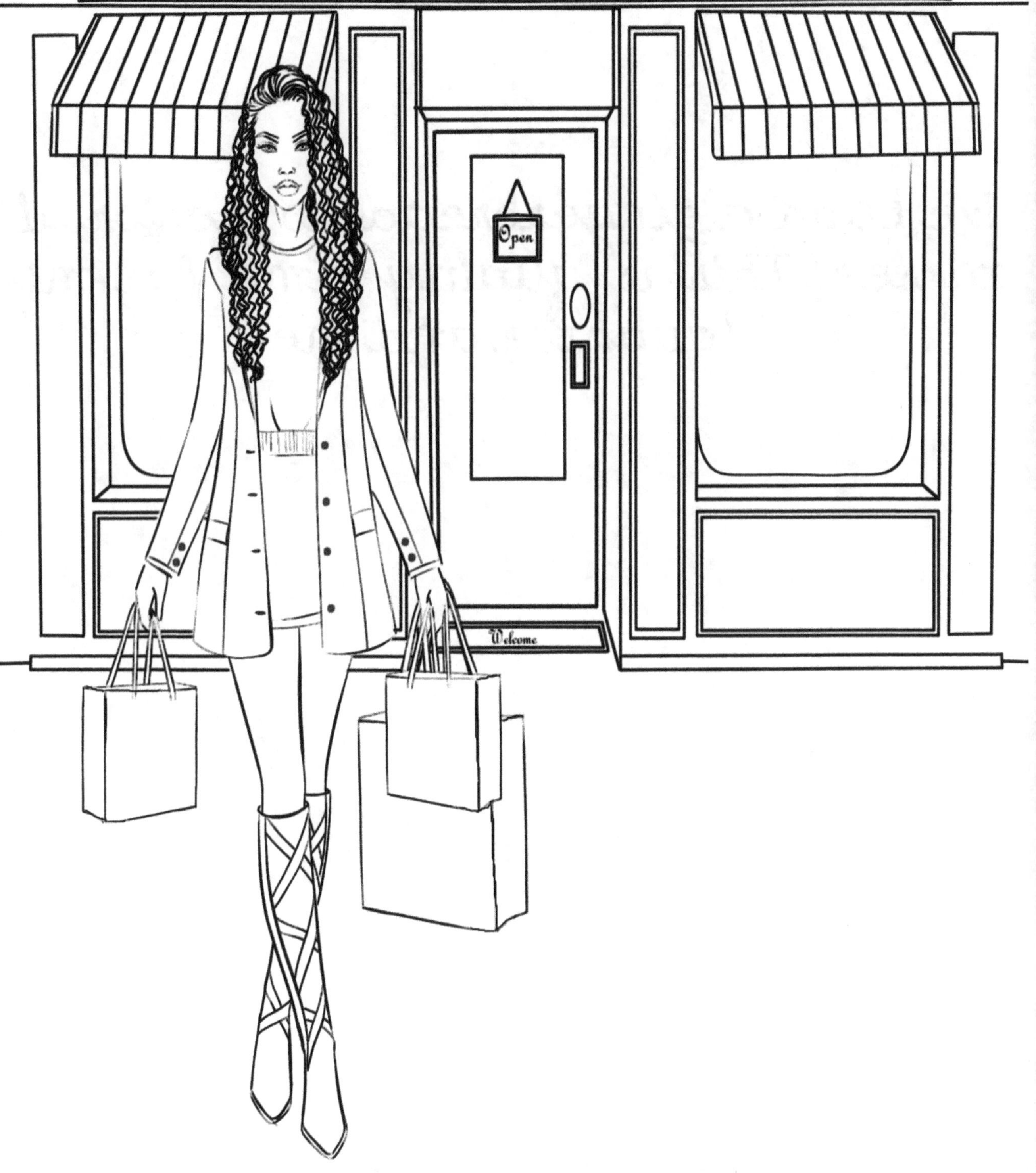

CHRISTMAS SALE UP TO 50% OFF
Boutique
Open
Welcome
CHRISTMAS SALE UP TO 50% OFF

We build a gingerbread house for all to see. This is quality time for my daughter and me!

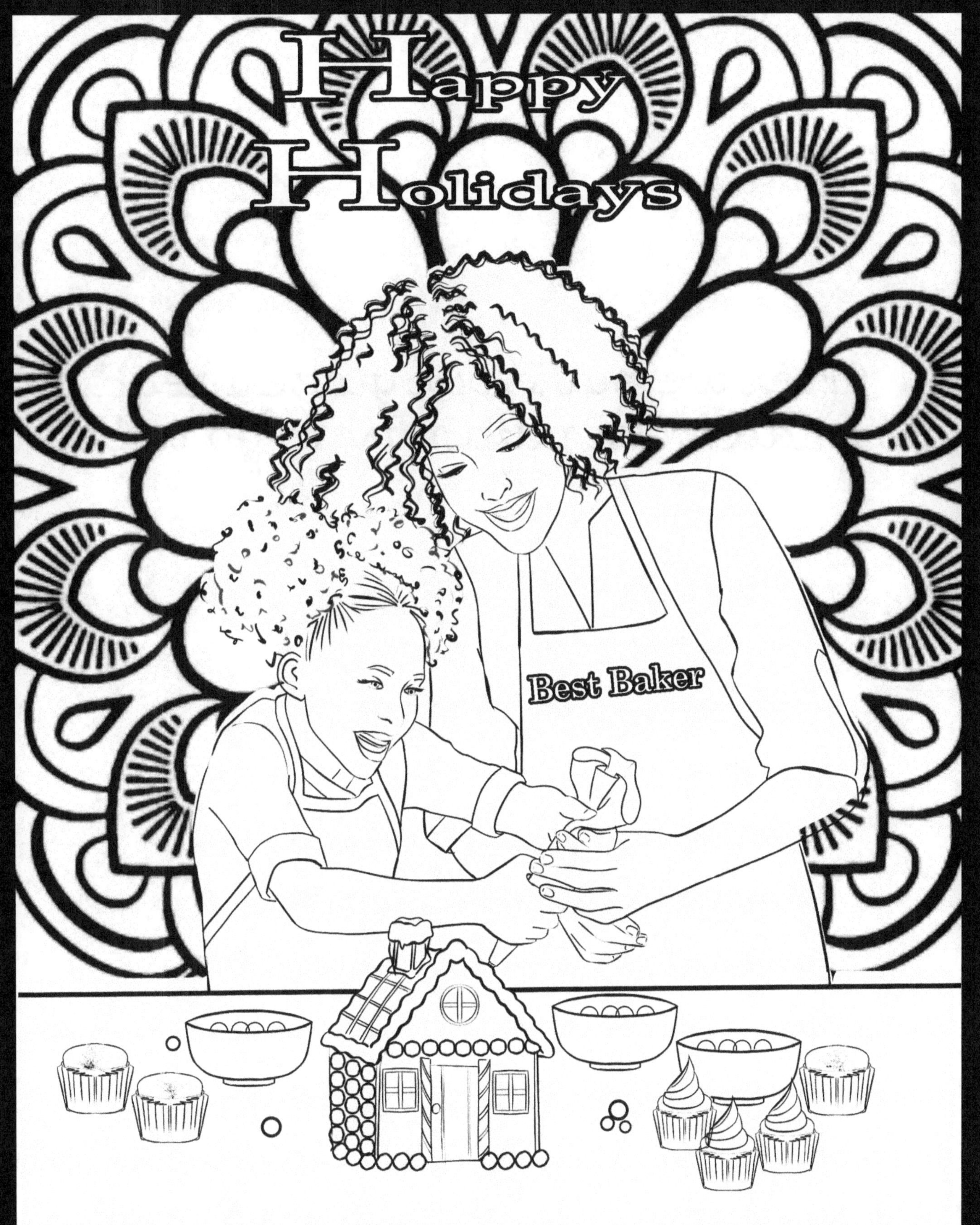

Happy
Holidays
Best Baker

After we make our gingerbread,
We match our pajamas to go to bed.

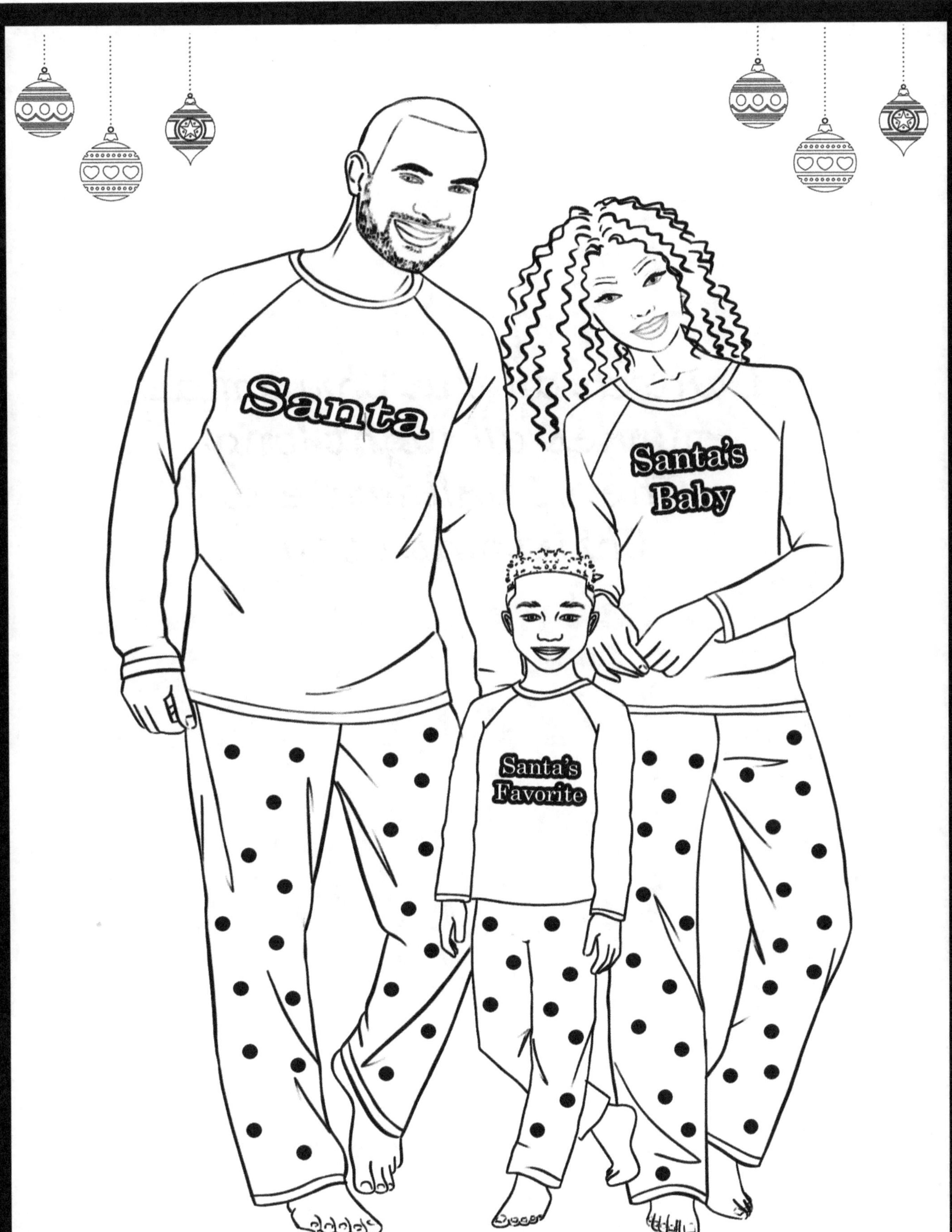

Santa
Santa's Baby
Santa's Favorite

I watch all the Christmas movies all night long. Then I will write a Christmas song!

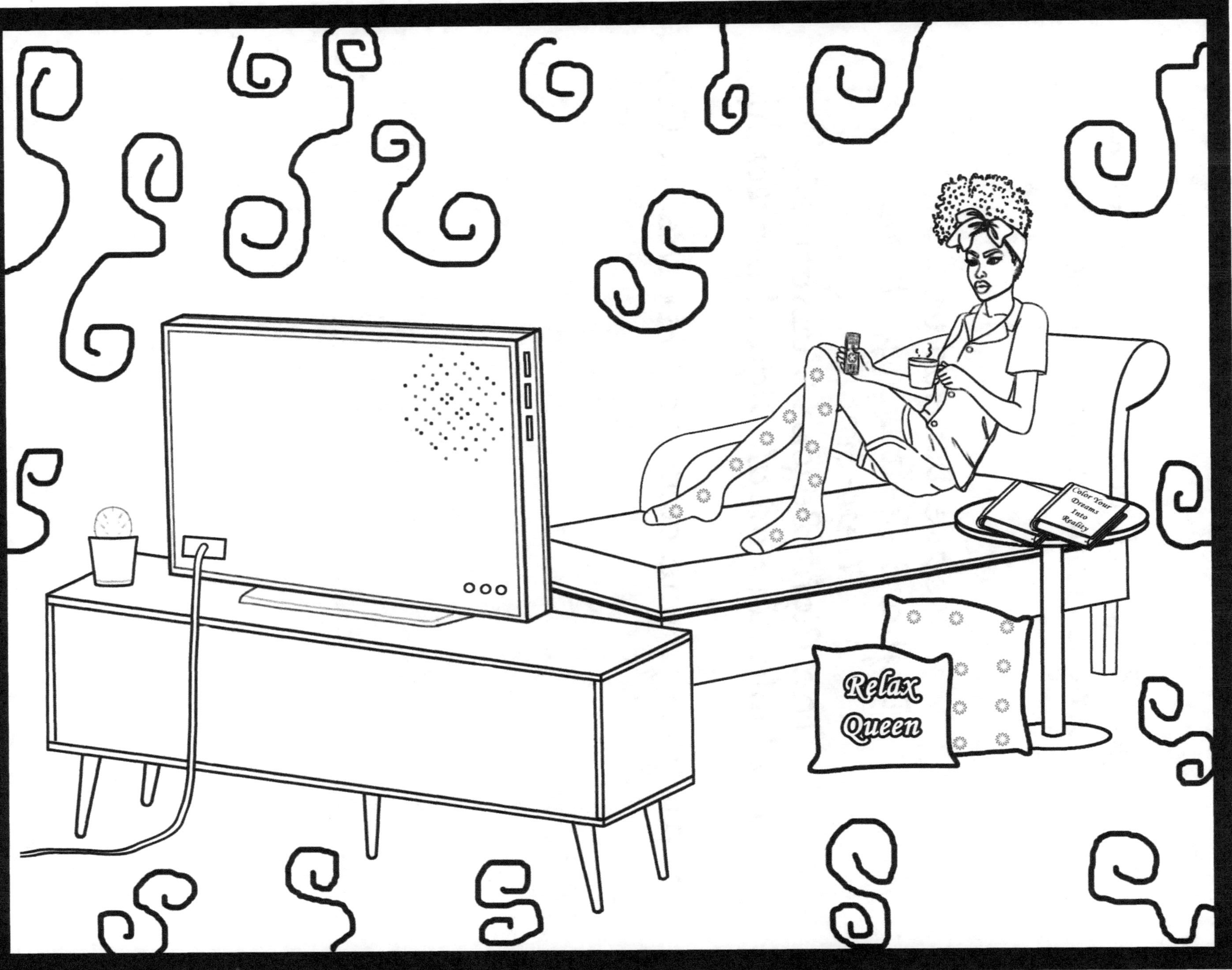

Color Your Dreams Into Reality
Relax Queen

The Night Before Christmas with Allure. Our song is now in digital stores.

Please Download
Dejha B Featuring. Allure
New Single
"The Night Before Christmas"
Available now on all Digital platforms

Scan your phone camera over the QR Code.

The Night Before Christmas

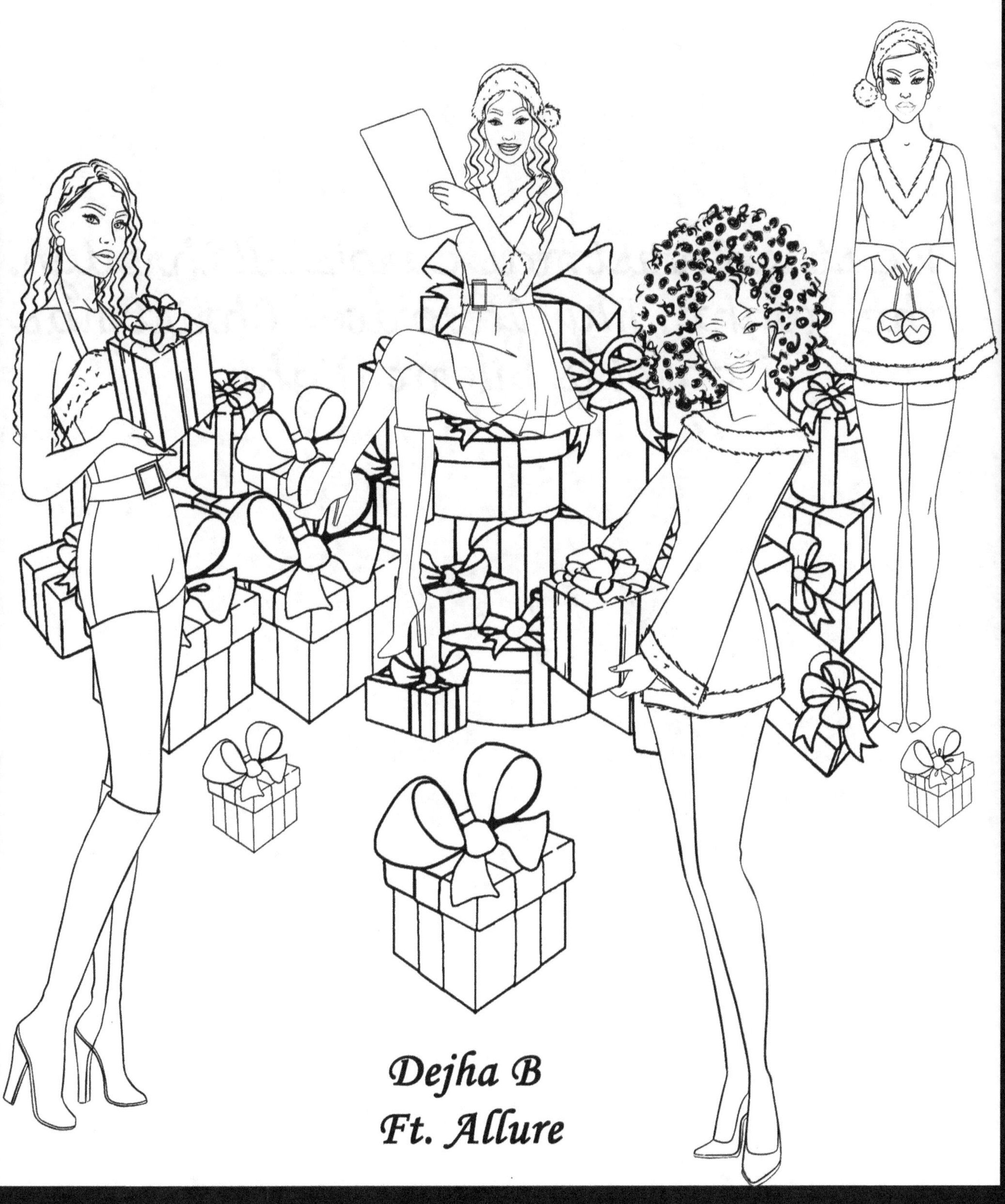

Dejha B
Ft. Allure

We sing Christmas carols all through the night. My favorite Christmas carol is Silent Night.

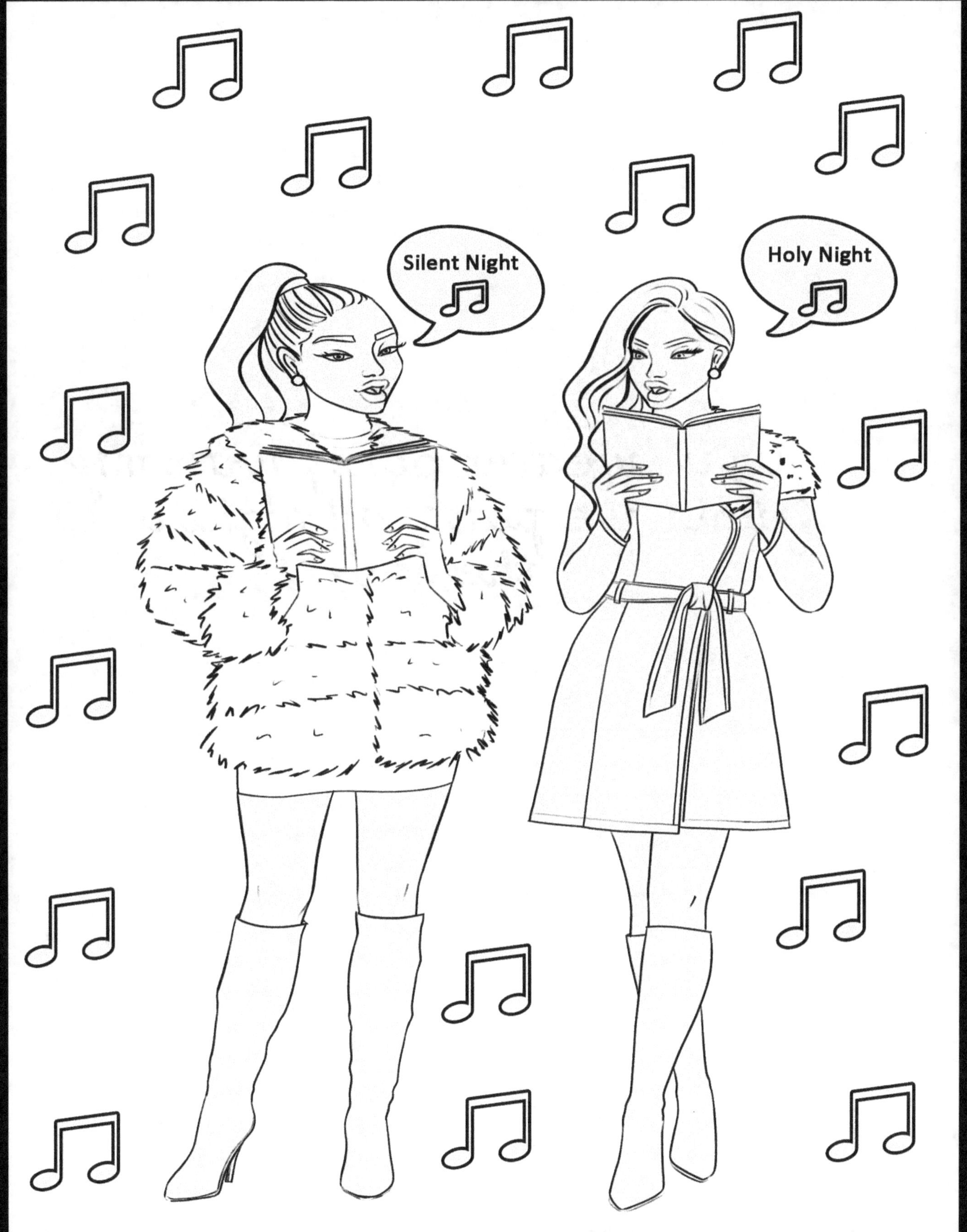

Silent Night
Holy Night

Ugly sweater party with my friend, we party all night until the end!

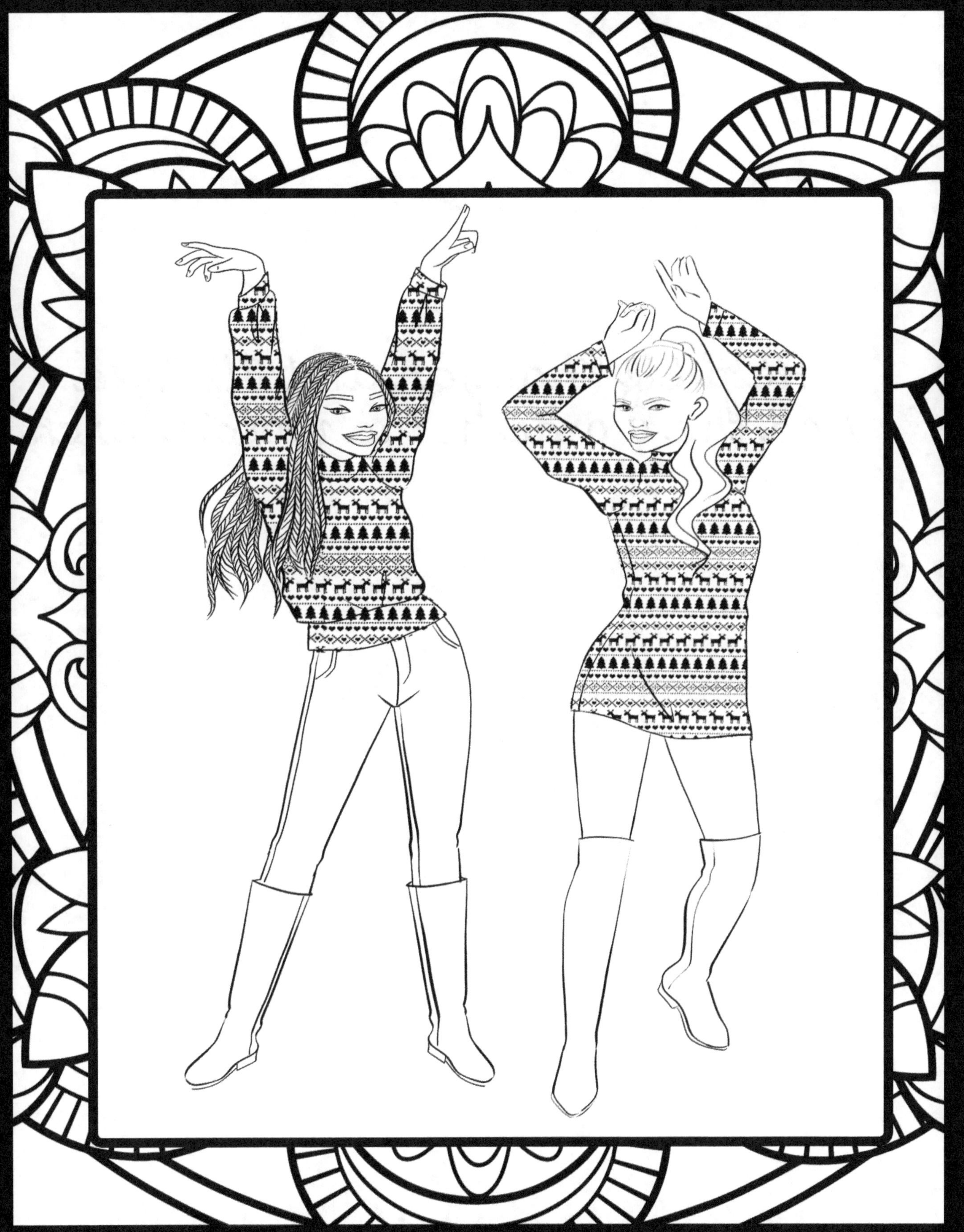

Help Elf Khaliyah and Elf Nyla
find the words in the word search

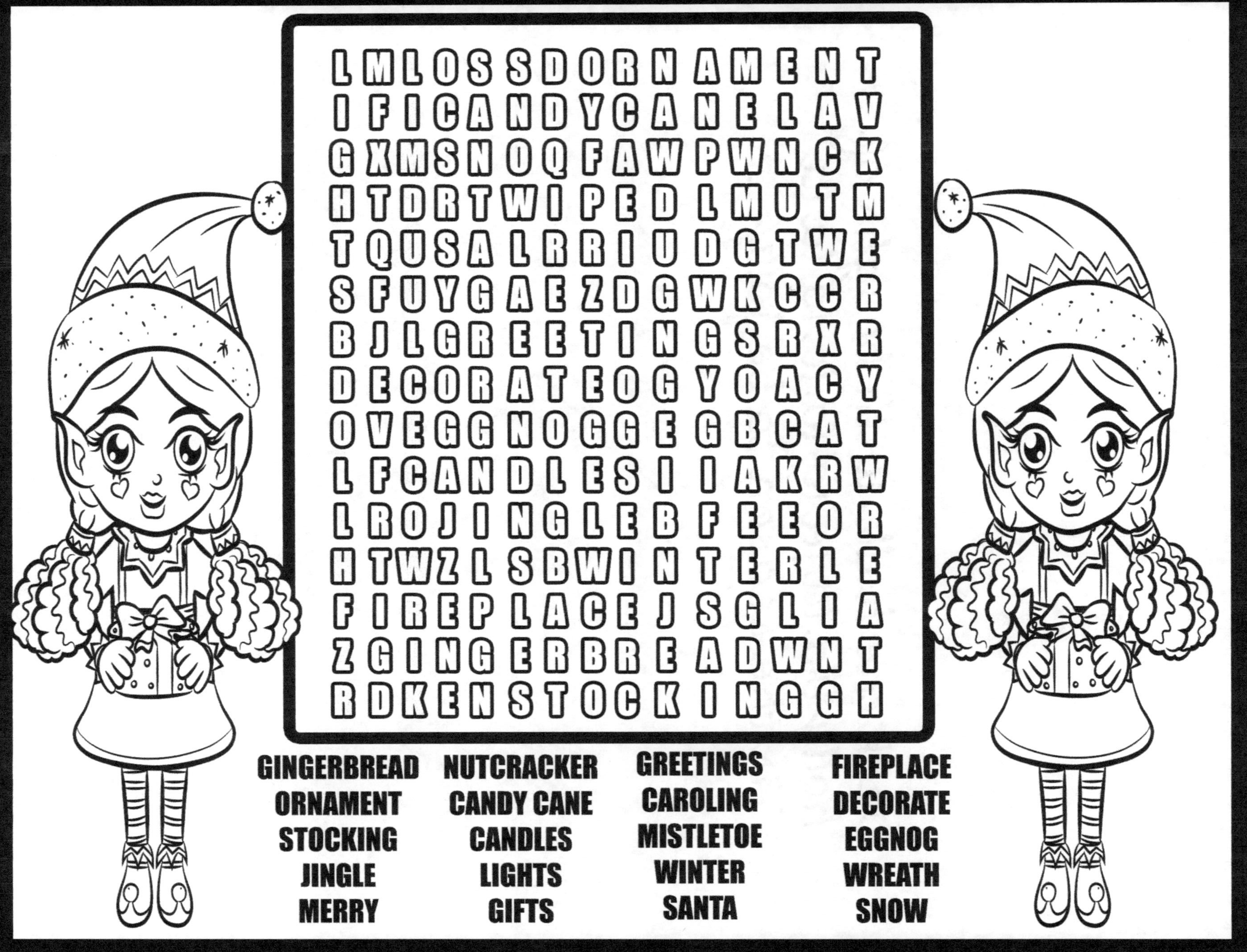

L M L O S S D O R N A M E N T
I F I C A N D Y C A N E L A V
G X M S N O Q F A W P W N C K
H T D R T W I P E D L M U T M
T Q U S A L R R I U D G T W E
S F U Y G A E Z D G W K C C R
B J L G R E E T I N G S R X R
D E C O R A T E O G Y O A C Y
O V E G G N O G G E G B C A T
L F C A N D L E S I I A K R W
L R O J I N G L E B F E O R E
H T W Z L S B W I N T E R L E
F I R E P L A C E J S G L I A
Z G I N G E R B R E A D W N T
R D K E N S T O C K I N G G H

GINGERBREAD   NUTCRACKER   GREETINGS   FIREPLACE
ORNAMENT   CANDY CANE   CAROLING   DECORATE
STOCKING   CANDLES   MISTLETOE   EGGNOG
JINGLE   LIGHTS   WINTER   WREATH
MERRY   GIFTS   SANTA   SNOW

Deck the halls with boughs of holly Fa la la la la la la la la. Tis the season to be jolly........

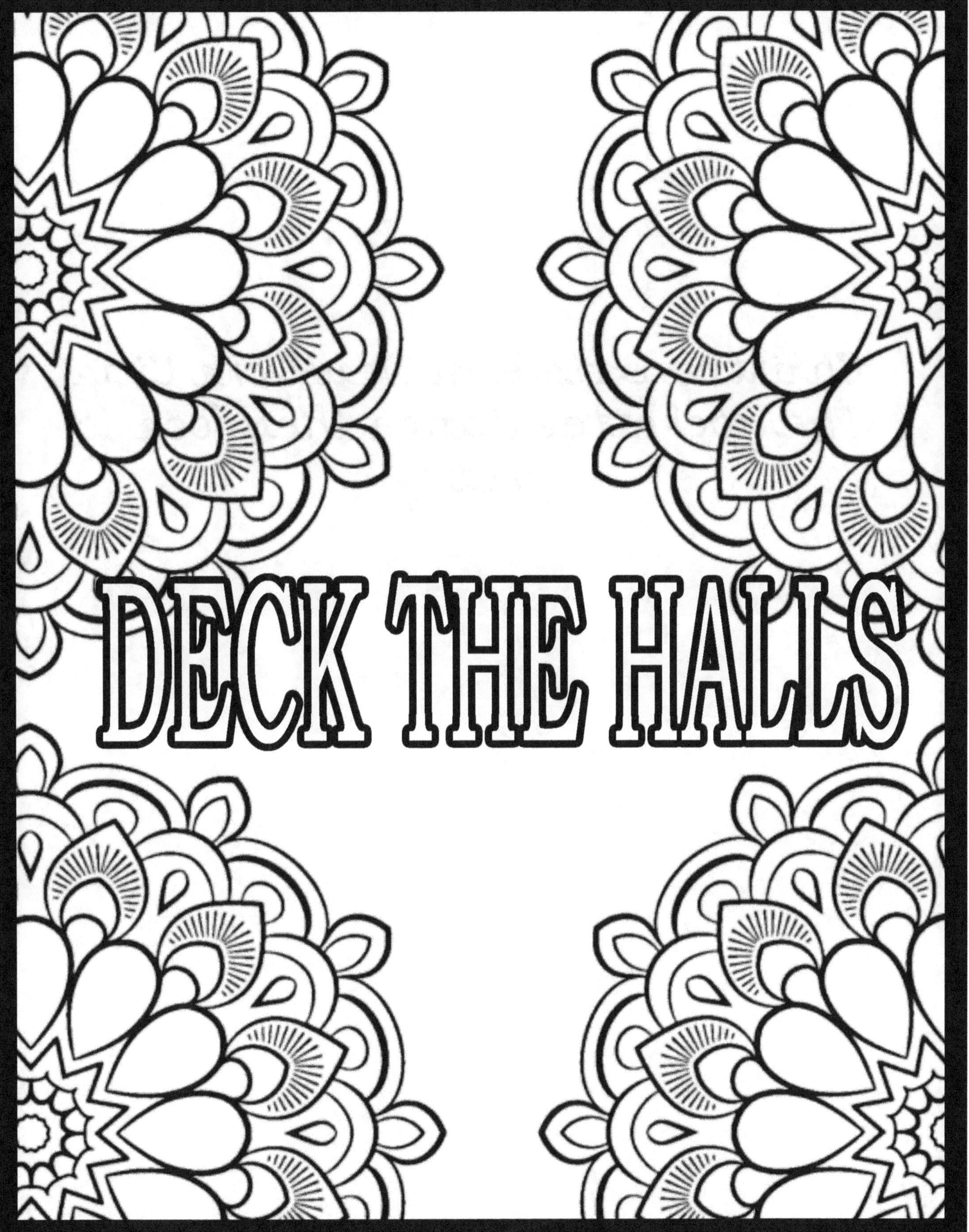

DECK THE HALLS

Christmas time in New York City. The Rockettes dance they look so pretty.

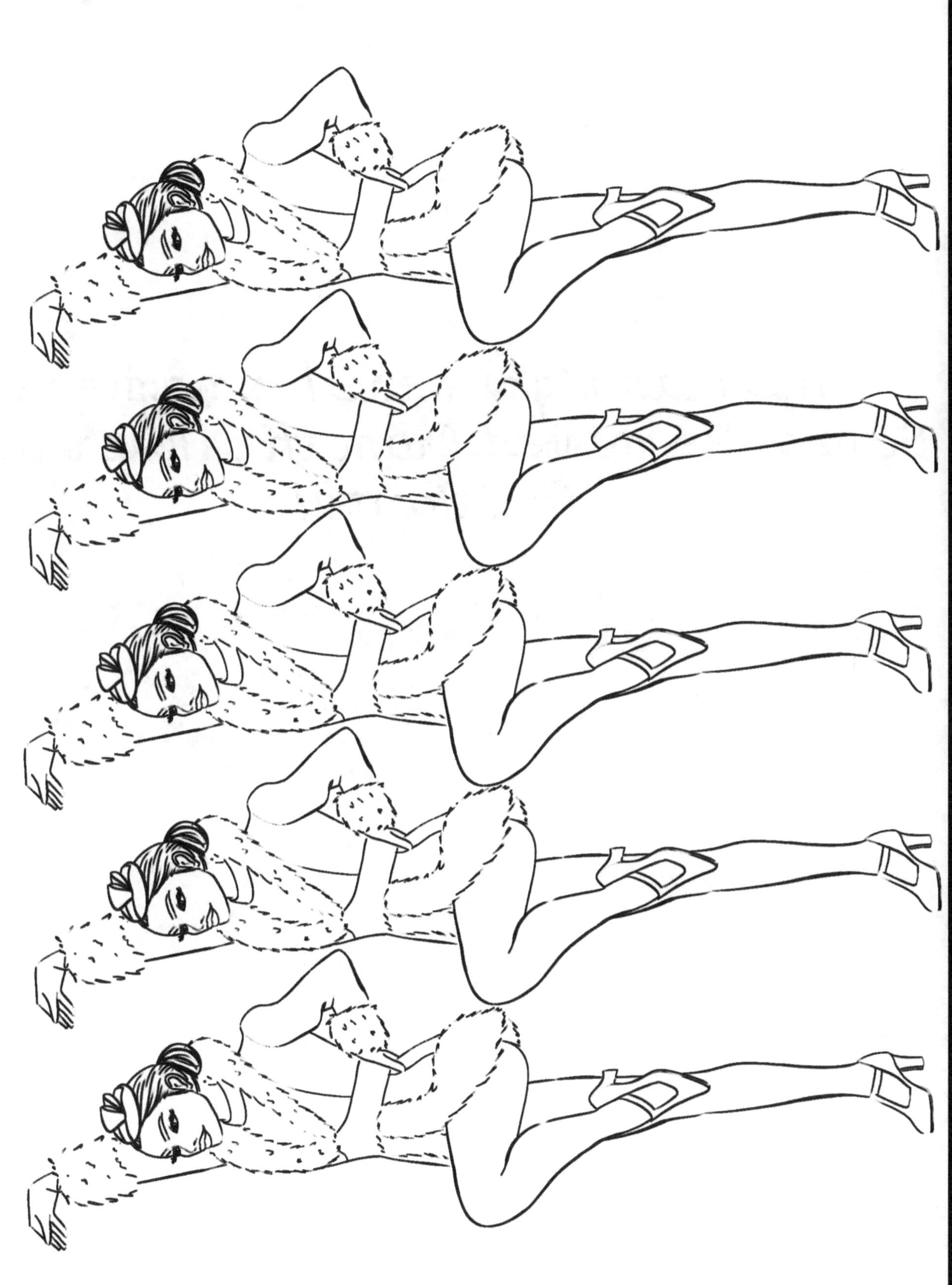

This man right here his name is
Santa.. He moved from the North pole
to Atlanta!

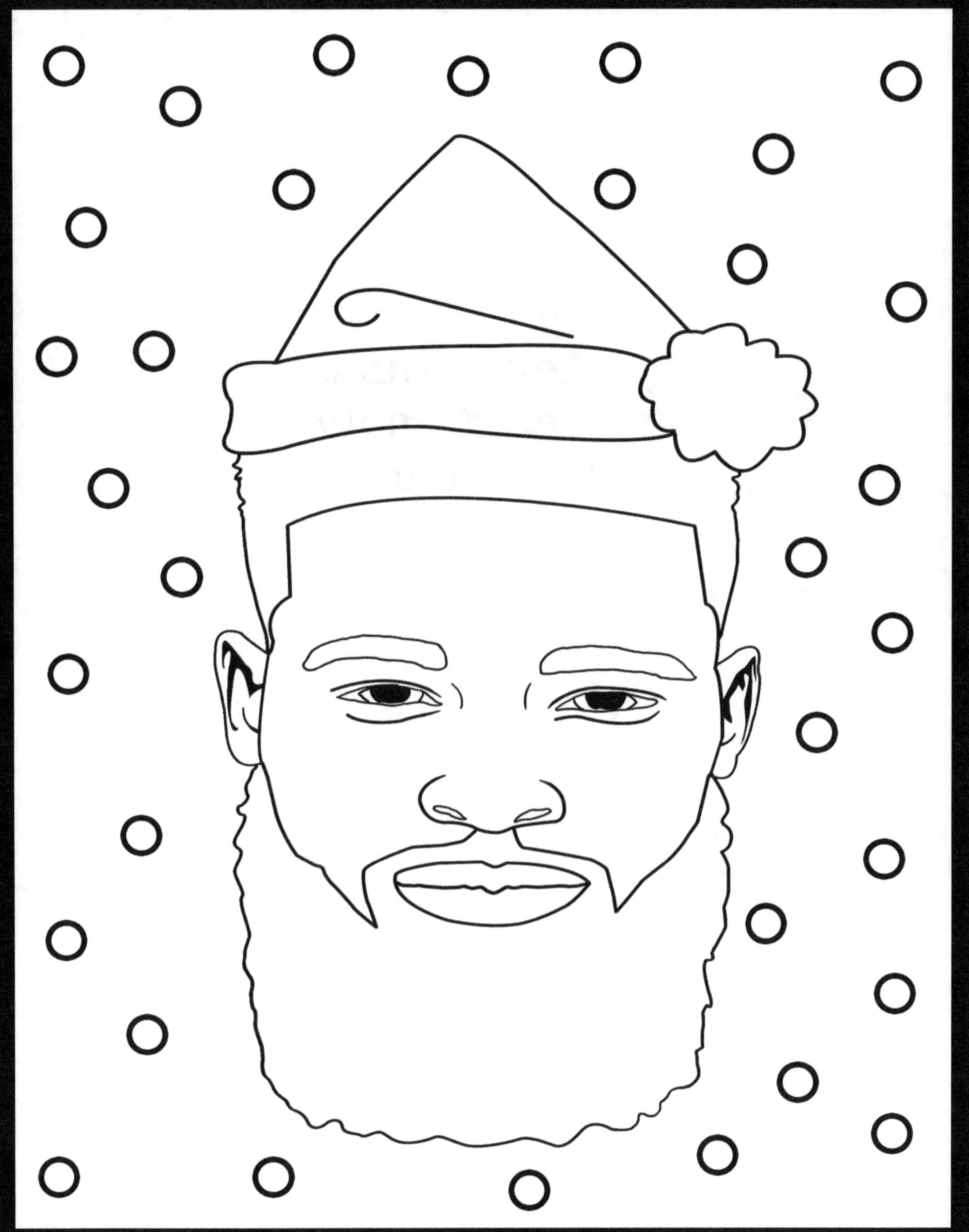

Let it snow
Let it snow
Let it snow.....

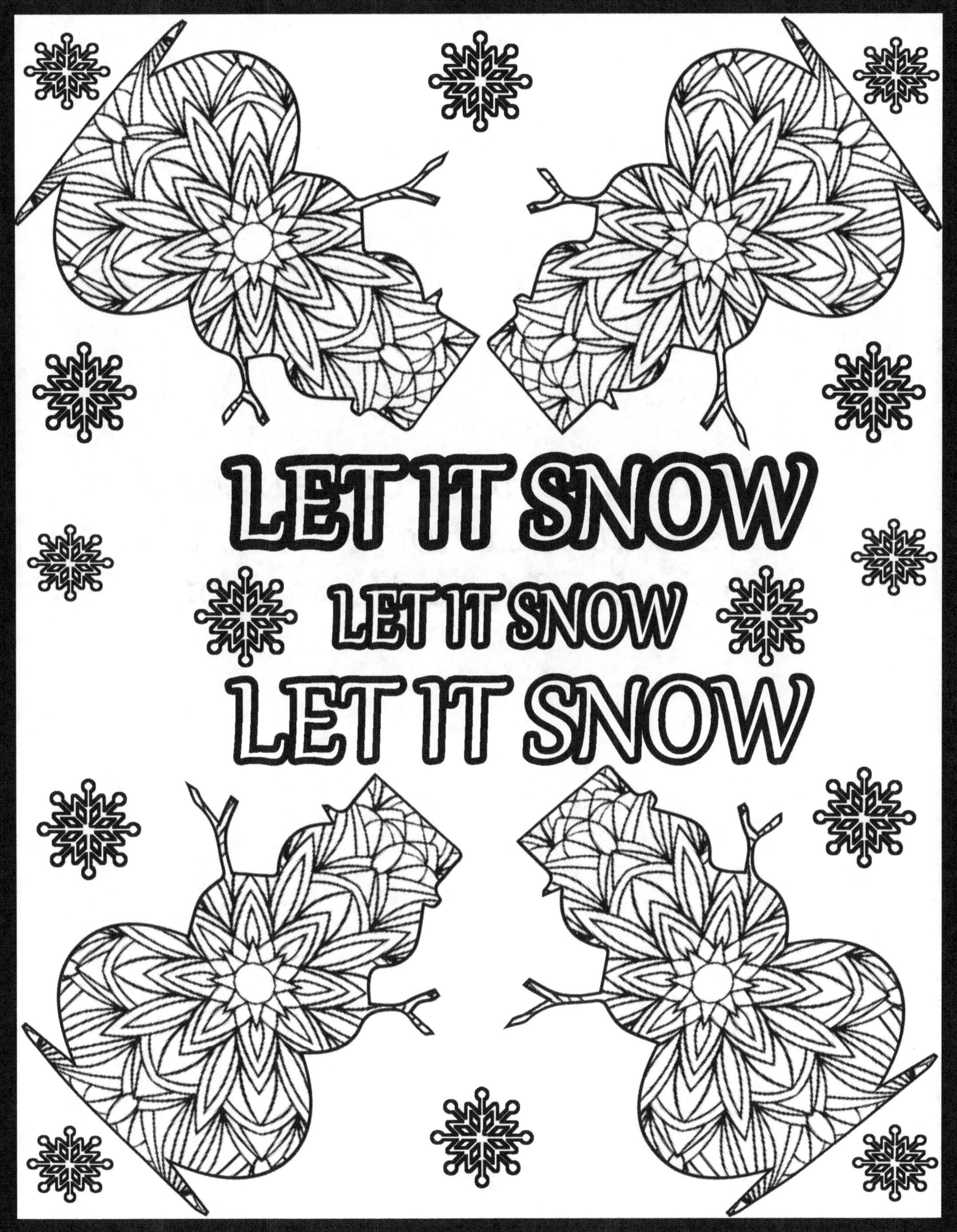

LET IT SNOW
LET IT SNOW
LET IT SNOW

I'll bake some cookies that
are soft and hot. I'll eat the
cookies I love them alot.

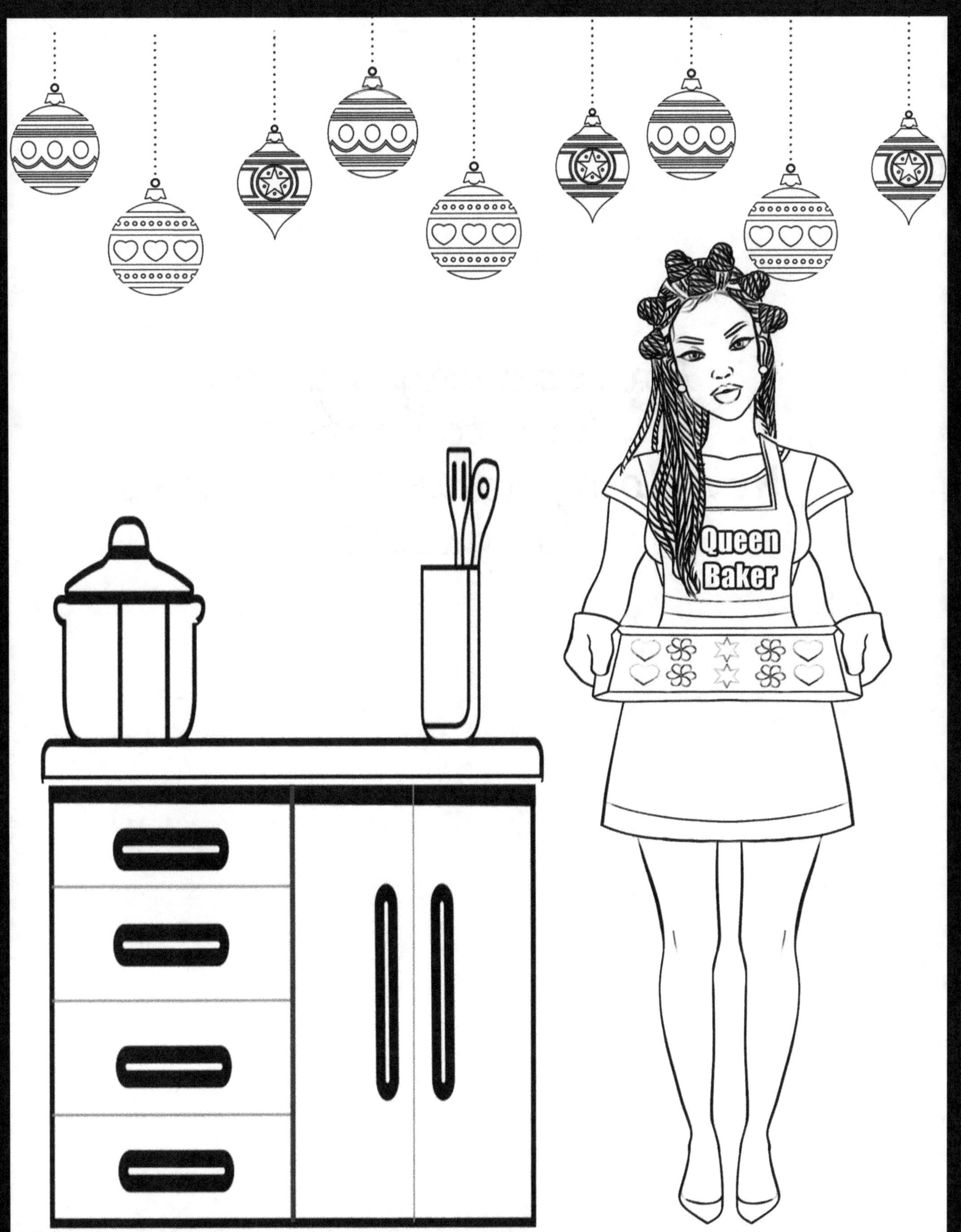

Queen
Baker

I'm teaching my son
how to skate.
He's doing so well he skates
so great!

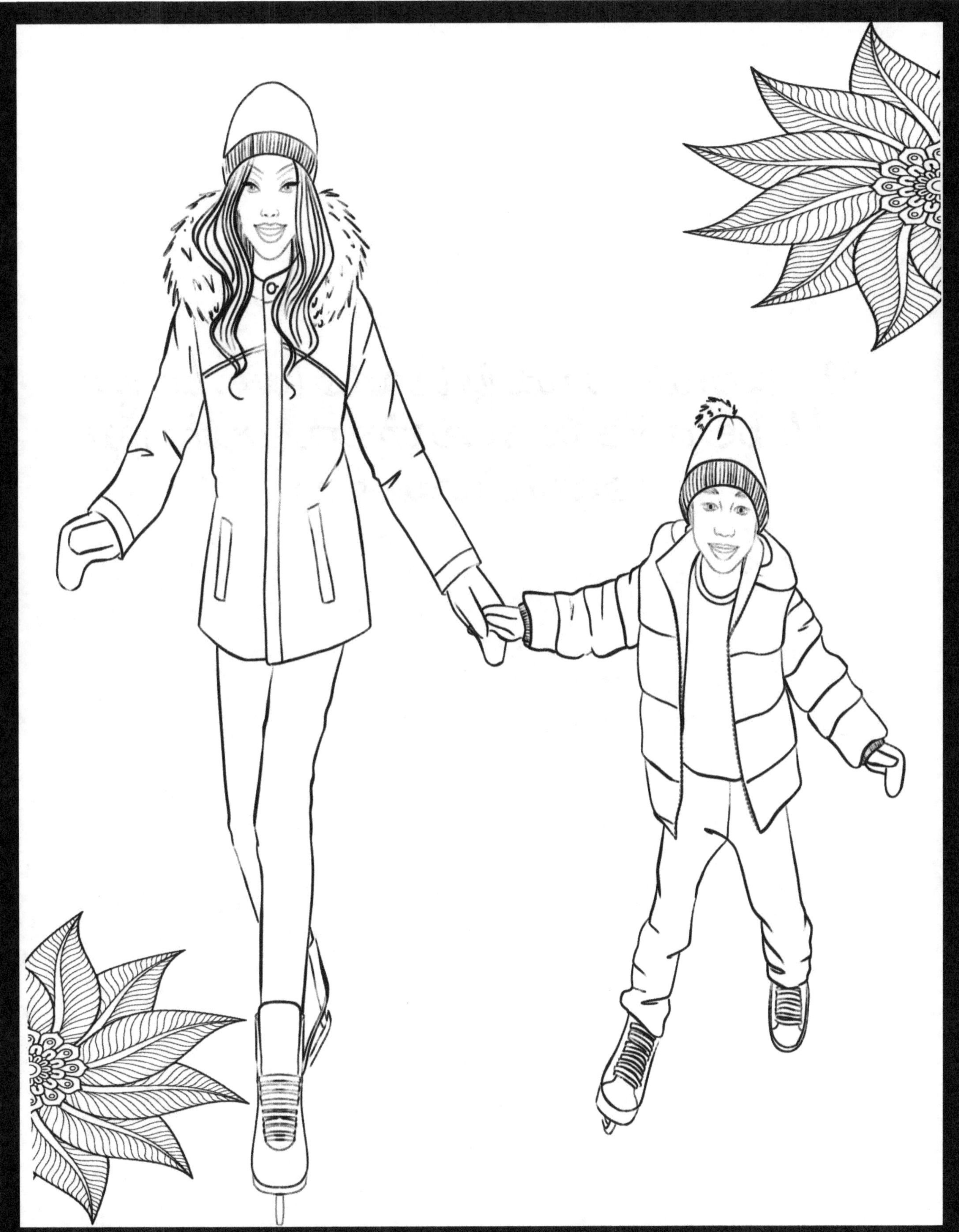

My family and friends live so far.
I'll be able to see them with my
brand new car.

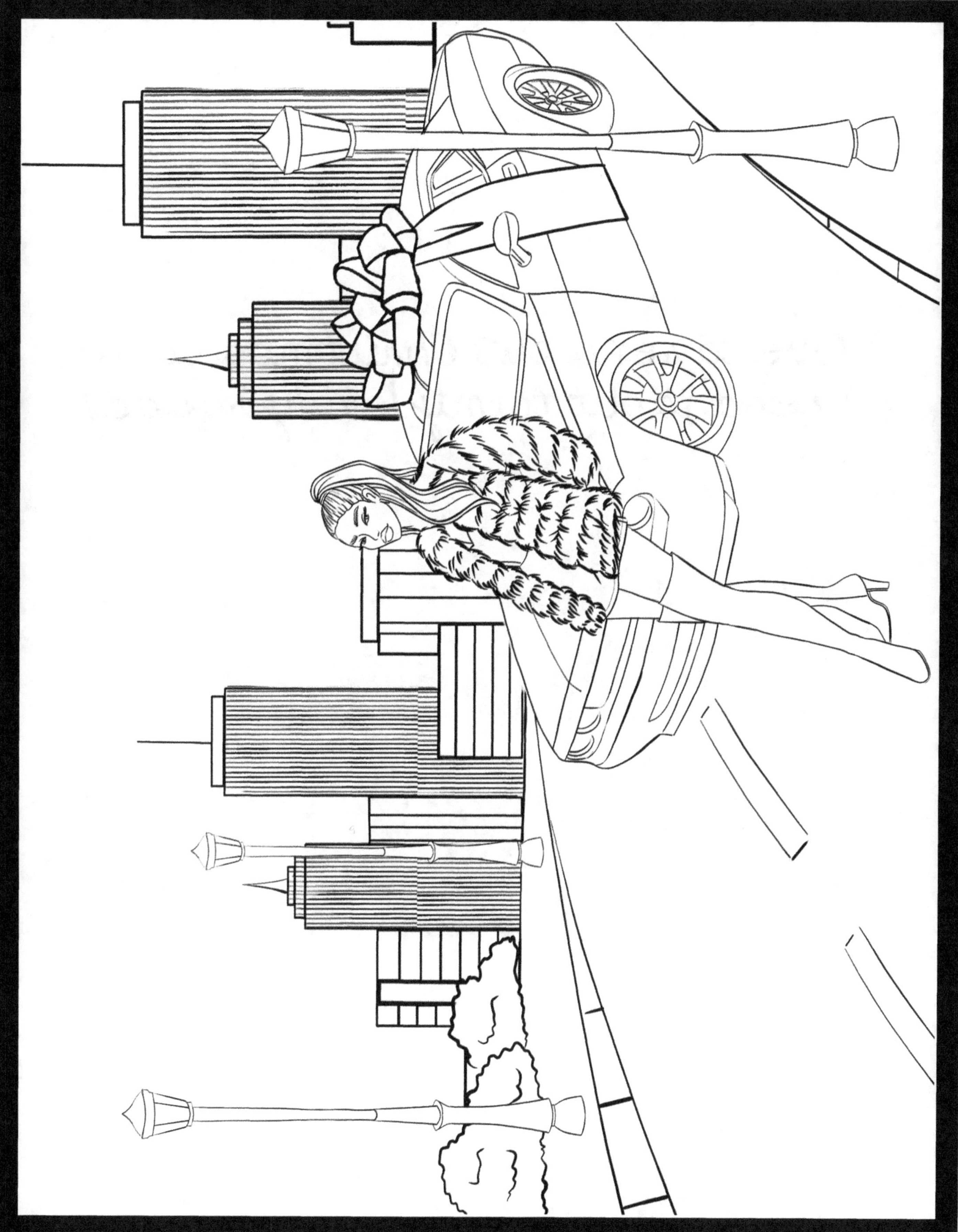

I love to send out Christmas cards.
I send it out to my lovely squad!

Peace
Family
Traditions
Joy
Love
Peace
Friends
Love
Peace
Family

I love to give out Christmas gifts and grant everyone their Christmas wish!

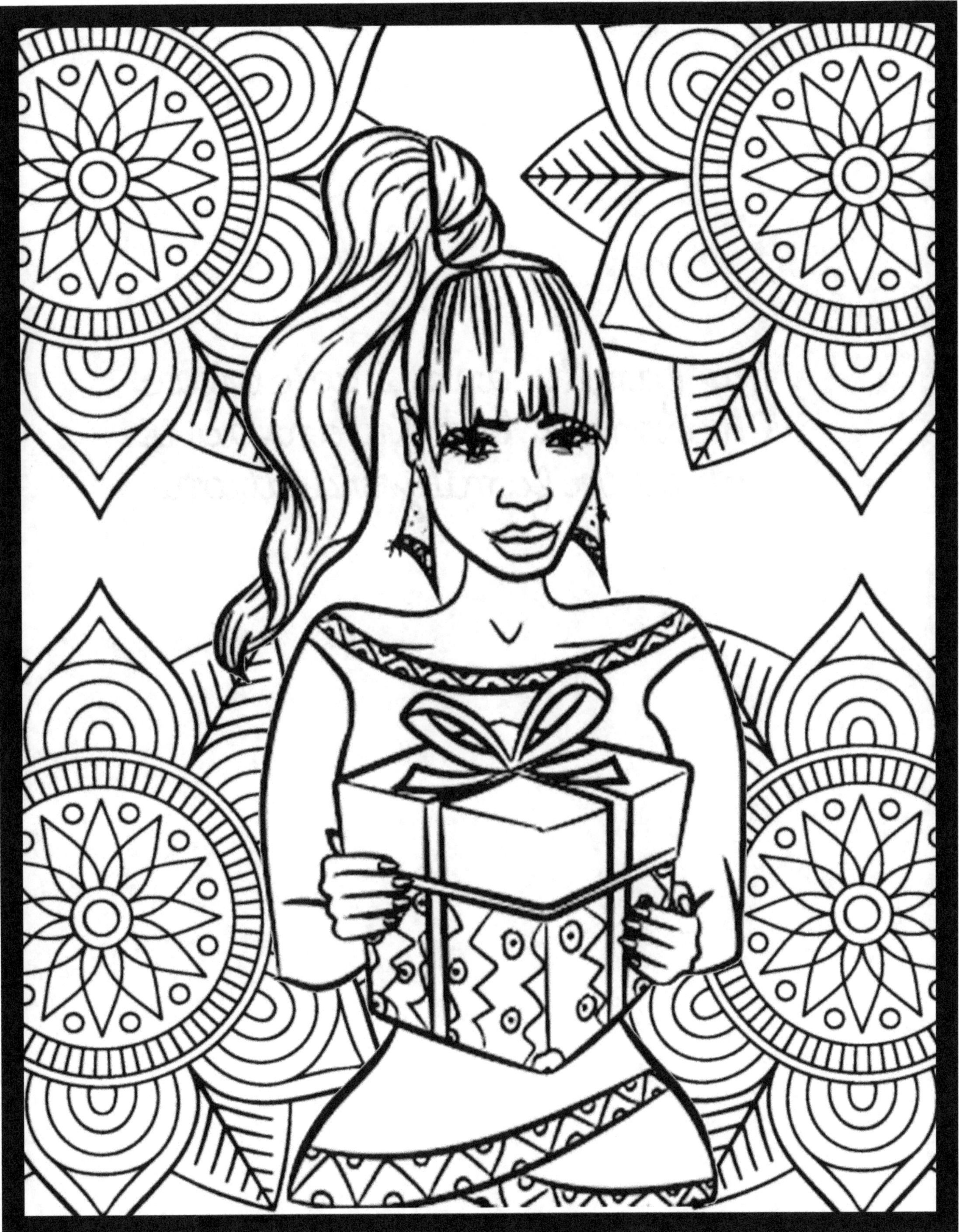

My family and I celebrate
Christmas, but Kwanzaa is
also our family tradition.

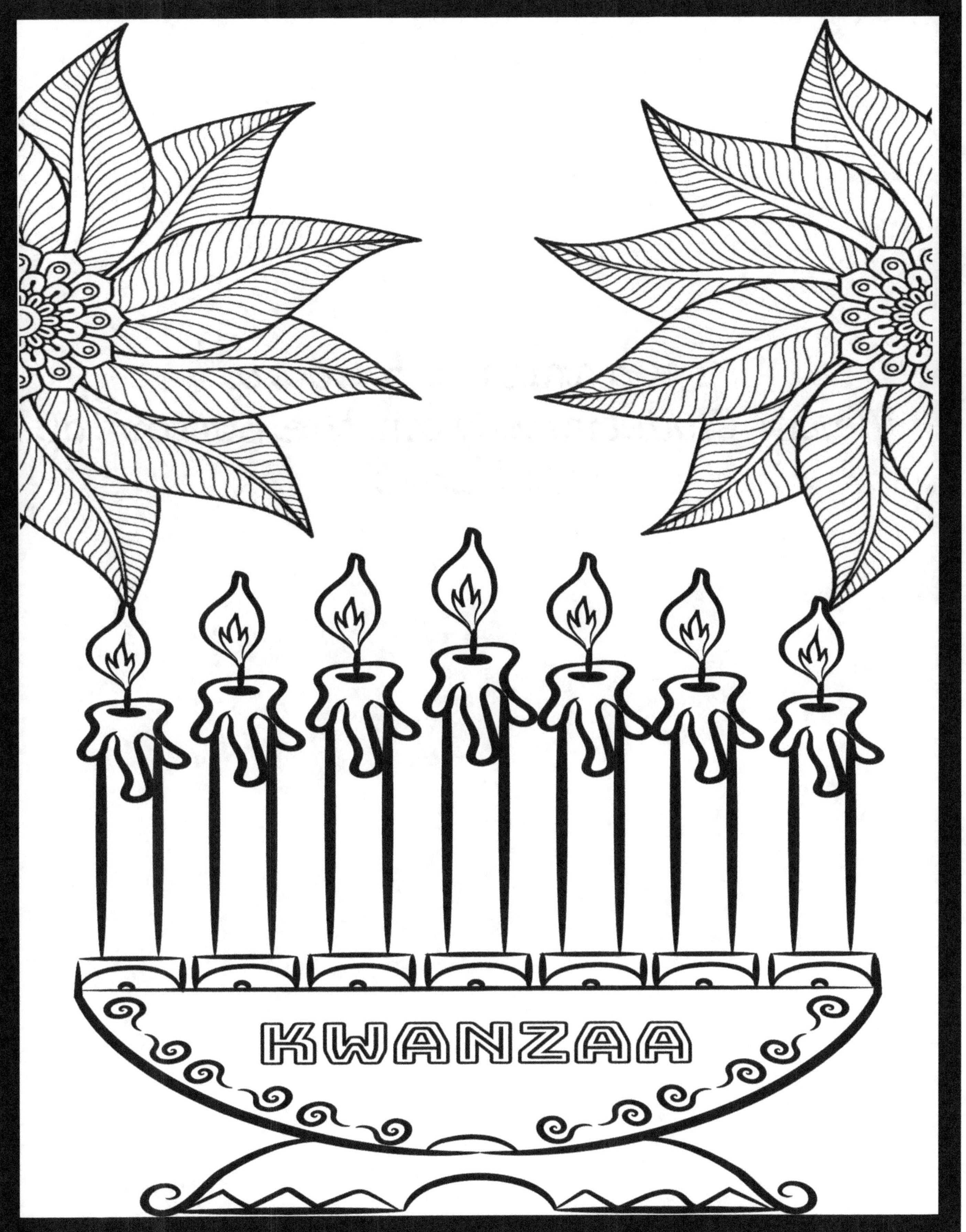

KWANZAA

I wanna wish you a
Merry Christmas from the bottom of
my heart....

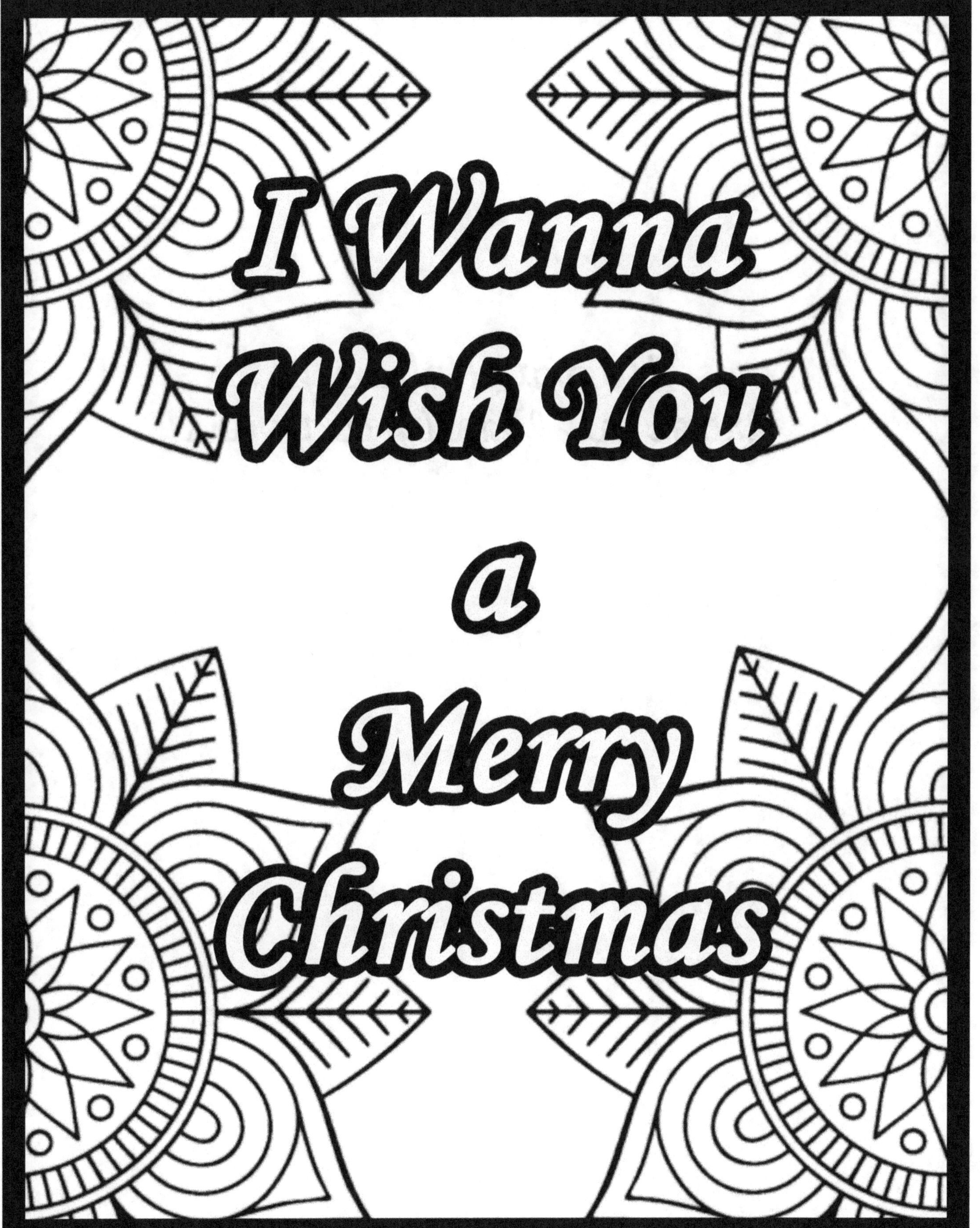

I Wanna
Wish You
a
Merry
Christmas

Happy Holidays
from my family to yours!

HAPPY HOLIDAYS

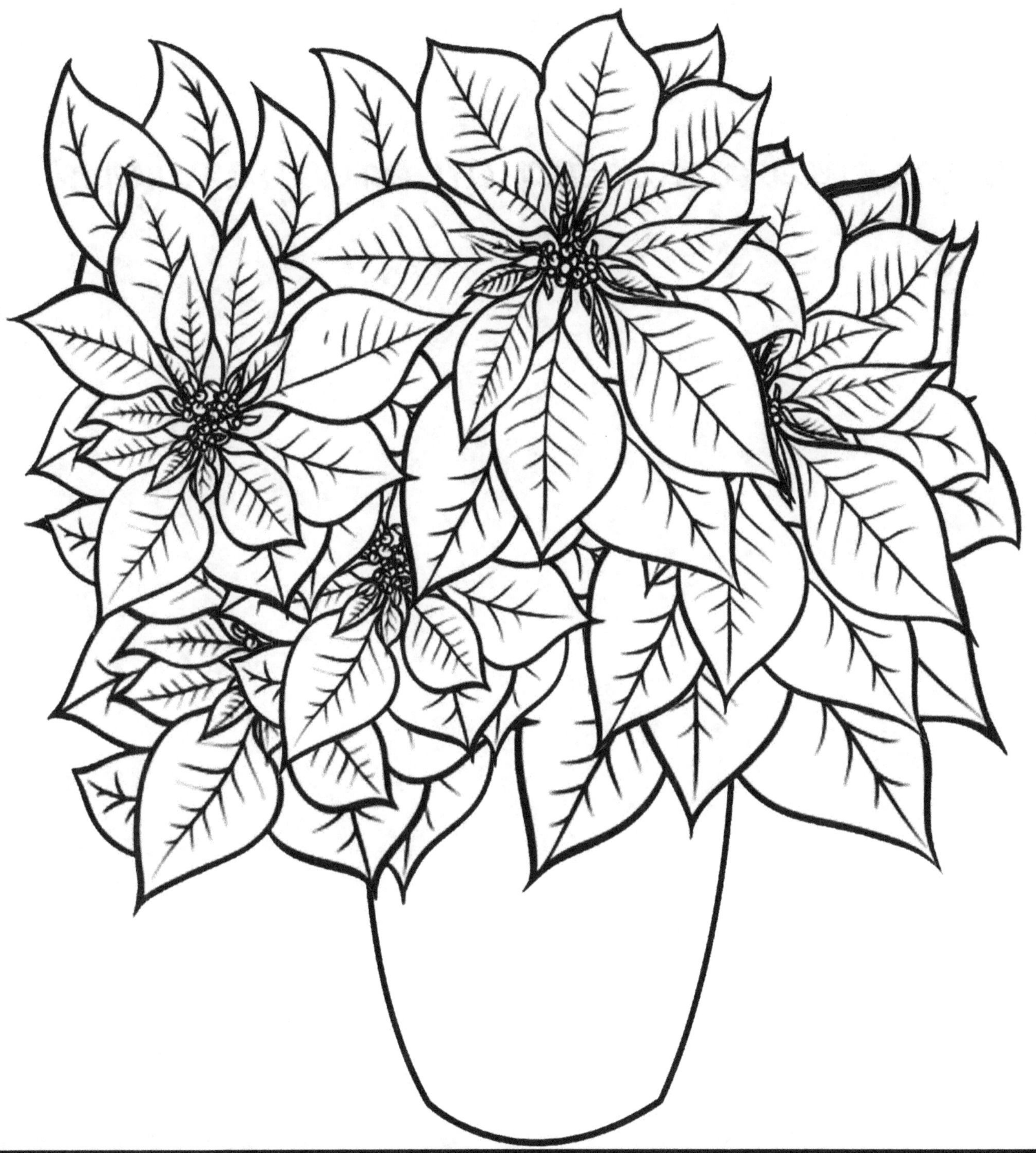

Chestnut roasting on an open fire!

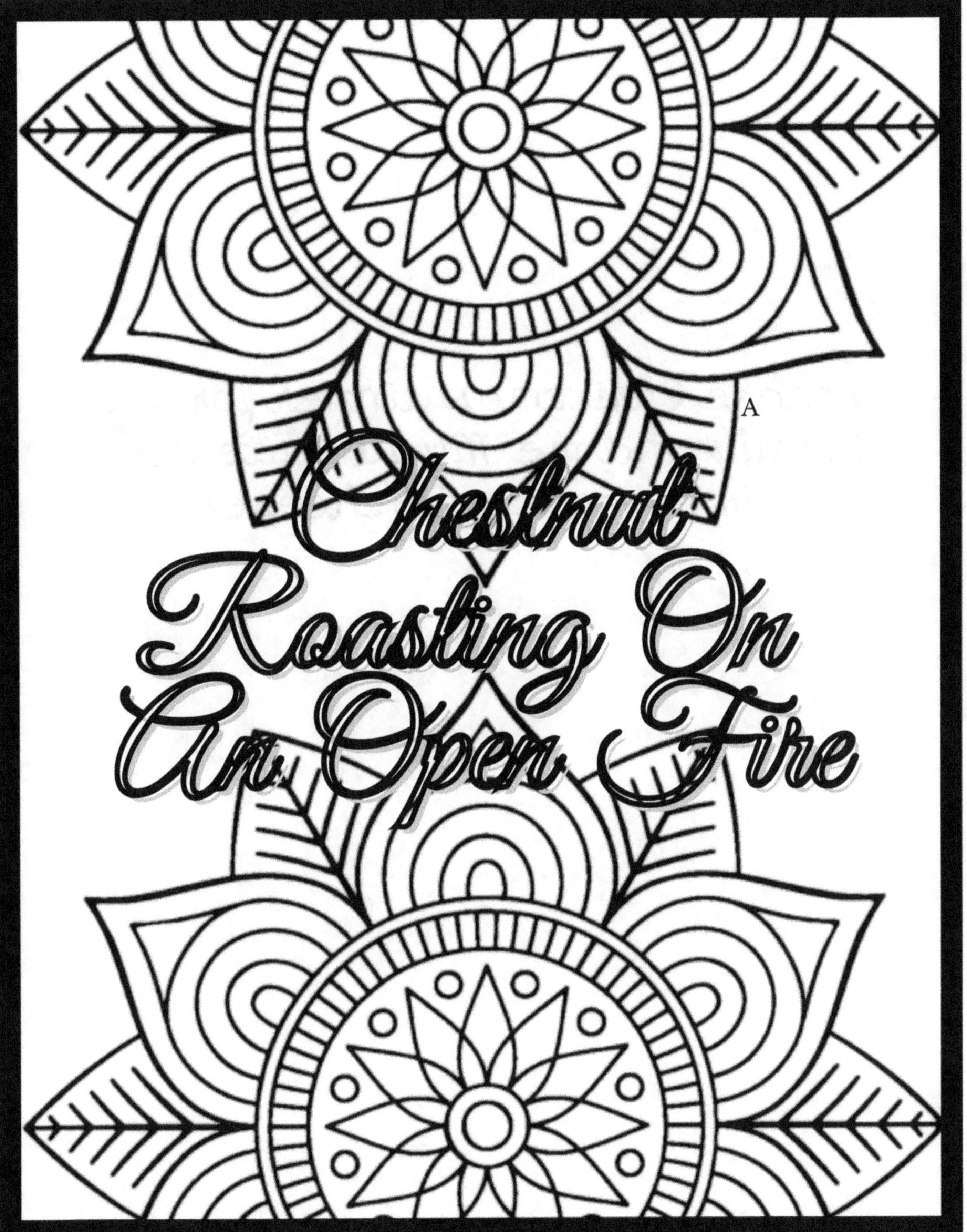

Chestnut Roasting On An Open Fire

I make Christmas dinner for my family and me. My favorite dish is my mac and cheese!

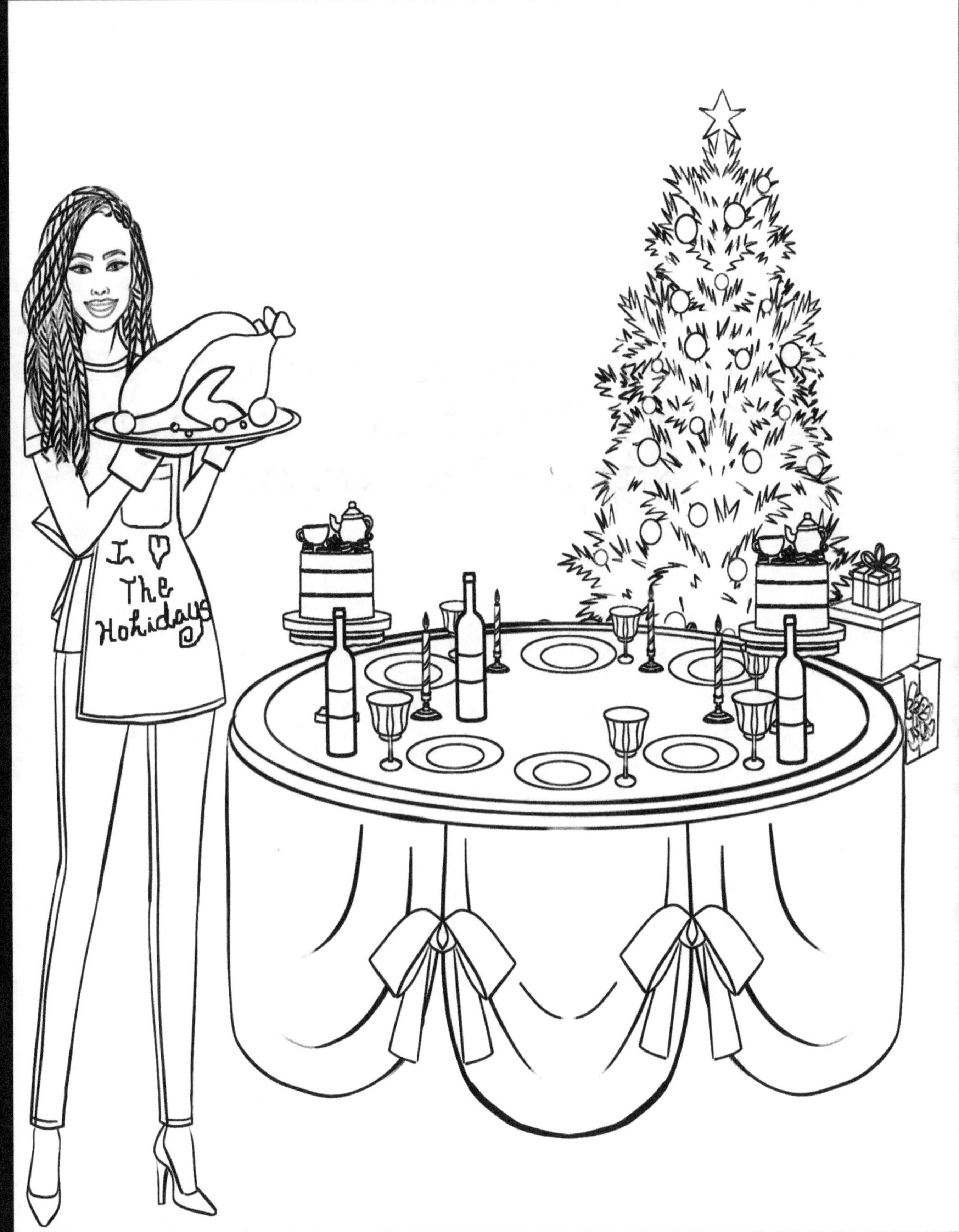

I ♥ The Holidays

It's the most wonderful time of the year. Merry Christmas and have a Happy New Year!

IT'S THE MOST
WONDERFUL TIME
OF THE YEAR
Merry Christmas

Wishing You A Colorful Christmas

I hope you have a wonderful Christmas.

For more coloring books visit
www.dejhabcoloring.com

Please Follow the brand "Dejha B Coloring" social media pages:

Instagram and Facebook pages @DejhaBColoring and tag your coloring pages.
Use Hashtag #DejhaBColoring

Please join "DejhaBColoring" Facebook Group to share your coloring pages.

Please follow "Black Angel Publishing" social media pages for more Inspirational books

Instagram: @BlackAngelPublishing
Facebook Page: www.facebook.com/BlackAngelPublishing

Follow the Creator/Author Dejha B
Instagram: @iamdejhab2
www.iamdejhab.com
Facebook Page: www.facebook.com/iamdejhab2

Test Your Coloring Tools On This Page.